FROM SECRETARY
TO STRIPPER

AMY BECKETT

PROLOGUE

I was born in the mid 1970s, in Maidstone, Kent, in England. My mother endured a 22-hour labour with me, during which and I quote:

"You ripped me to shreds and broke every blood vessel in both my eyes."

It mentally scarred my mother so she couldn't bond with me.

I went to live with her Mum and Dad, but when I was four years old, "Nanny" died of cancer, leaving my Granddad to raise me single-handedly. Granddad did the best he could, but the 51-year age gap was difficult for he and I at times. He often raised his voice to me and I cried a lot – sometimes I didn't even know why.

Family disagreements before Nanny died resulted in me not really seeing my mother much and when I did, I found it hard to get along with her and my younger siblings as I was basically brought up as an only child. But that didn't mean that I didn't love or miss Mum when she wasn't around. I just didn't know how to gel with her, nor her with me. I was the only girl she had and I often wondered if maybe me being a girl was one of the reasons she decided she didn't want me around. She also seemed to get on better with people of the male gender like I did. My excuse was being brought up by a man. I'm not sure what hers was.

I was a very lonely child. My Daddy became untraceable in Spain in the late '80s and I didn't manage to track him down again until the Summer of 1997. After going through another divorce and not feeling too great about himself, he'd decided I was better off just being taken care of by my Granddad. I was so angry with him for making that decision because in my eyes it wasn't his to make. Every year I waited in vain hope I'd get a birthday card from him. Every year nothing came and I cried with disappointment.

Being an "only child" meant that I had a lot of time on my hands. I would read encyclopaedias and nonfiction books to saturate my brain with trivia. I remember when I was seven I would look through the classified sections of the newspapers. I was mesmerised at the little ad boxes with pictures of women wearing sexy lingerie and stockings and suspenders, and beside them the words "kissograms/stripagrams." I wanted to be one. I wanted to look good, sexy (even though I didn't really know what "sexy" meant then) and be liked/loved/adored. Why I thought wearing sexy lingerie would do that for me I have no idea. I didn't tell any adults my ambitions, but I would tell people at school:

"I want to be a kissogram/stripper" and from time to time "I want to be a model or a singer."

1
THE BEGINNING

L et me introduce myself.

Well, I'll introduce myself to you as the persona I once was. Once upon a time, I was known as Holly Burnett. And I used to be a somebody. A somebody to many involved and interested in the "glamour" world, AKA the "adult entertainment industry".

I say I *used to be* a somebody; I'm still a somebody now, just to different people – to friends and family, to myself. No longer to a bunch of strangers I seek validation from. A somebody who looks back and at times finds it hard to associate herself with that old persona. At times it seems like "she" was a completely different person. Looking back, I feel like I'm on the outside looking in. But that's not a bad thing.

Times change and so do people. But people are fascinated in the industry I chose to be in. Fascinated because they want to know why we choose it, why we live it, what goes on behind the scenes and how, if at all, it affects our personal and private lives.

So let's begin at the beginning...in 2001.

I was working locally as a Legal Secretary for a firm of solicitors. They allowed me flexitime as I needed a lot of time off to drive my Granddad to various hospital consultant and doctors' appointments. He had type 2 diabetes and Ménière's Disease. Some days I would work at the office as early as 7.30am, other times I would stay beyond 5pm. All us secretaries had keys to the office so we could let ourselves in whenever we wanted.

I had a best friend who also worked there – Amanda. She'd got me the job. We had lived together, worked together and went out together on weekends. We'd recently fallen out due to being in each other's pockets all of the time and now the cracks were showing at work. Amanda played the victim and people always felt sorry for her. I did my job and left it at that, but she helped to make my working life hell. The accounts department were great friends with her and kept moving my files to the bottom of the pile so they came back after everyone else's; then I would get questioned by the solicitor I worked for as to why my work was so late. After an argument with Amanda one night I received threatening calls and voicemails from some random guy, followed by nuisance calls and heavy breathers on my home phone all times of day and night. I couldn't prove Amanda had anything to do with it, but I knew she did.

The situation was turning pretty awful. I started hating my job. Being a secretary wasn't really the best profession for me. I'd always wanted to be a performer or model of some kind, so I would buy a copy of *The Stage* Newspaper every week to see what jobs were on offer. As a secretary I felt like a goldfish in a bowl, watching the world go by through plate glass windows and feeling completely detached from the rest of the office. With that, a failed marriage behind me and my Granddad sick, I was feeling very low and I had started to see a counsellor.

One lunch hour I spotted a half-page advertisement in *The Stage*:

"Do you want to learn to pole dance?"

I couldn't believe my luck. A club in Mayfair, London was offering tuition for pole and table dancing. I called the number.

"We teach on Wednesdays, 6pm to 9pm. It's a three-week course. We have spaces for the next course which starts in two weeks. Would you like to attend?"

"Yes please," I said eagerly "can you post me the details?"

"Certainly," said the receptionist "and we'll see you then."

Working flexitime allowed me afternoons off to get into London for the course. I couldn't wait. I finally had something to look forward to.

The Wednesday arrived in November and I made my journey to London. There were a lot of girls waiting to go into the club. A few of us introduced ourselves to break the ice. We were split into groups of three; one group would start learning to dance tableside, one to pole dance and one to learn "dancer etiquette;" how to talk to customers. We learned each section for an hour then rotated, and there was *a lot* to learn. We discussed what we should and shouldn't say to gentlemen who come into the club, how to dance for them and how to remove our clothes without tripping over them. We were all impatient to take our turns on the pole; although without learning how to do a private dance and talk to customers, we knew we could never make money.

Once we had a hold of that pole we felt good about ourselves. We learned how to touch it, move up and down it, spin around it – all whilst wearing heels. Every week we learned more, emphasising our sexuality and gaining confidence. I would walk home from the train station feeling liberated and desirable.

The week before my last lesson in Mayfair I went to see my counsellor, crying about my office job, saying how much I hated it and how tired I was of all the problems due to Amanda. She suggested I request a week off work. I got the week off, even though the main partner of the solicitors really didn't want me to (he said he couldn't understand why I wasn't coping) and thought hard about what I really wanted. I enjoyed what I was learning in Mayfair, but was I good enough to work in a club?

On the final day of the course a lot of the students never showed up. I guess they realised being a table dancer wasn't for them. The manager of the club offered us all an audition. We had to dance to a song around the pole in a dress (standard club attire) whilst the manager watched and took notes. I decided to go for it. I got accepted, but was told to grow my hair (it was in a graduated bob), get a tan and lose weight on my behind.

The Beginning

Now I had to make a decision. Quit the solicitors and go to work in Mayfair full-time, or work both jobs part-time in case I wasn't cut out for dancing.

And then I received a letter from the solicitors office, explaining they thought it best not to renew my contract. I went to collect my things and just thought "someone up there/the universe has made the decision for me." The solicitors had actually done me a favour.

Years later, when I was looking for another part-time job to fill the gaps, that same firm of solicitors wrote me a bad reference, saying I hadn't been good at my job there. Funny that, considering even to this day I can still type over 70 words per minute and every other office I've worked at thought my work was impeccable. It's amazing how fickle people can be when they don't get their own way.

The day I cleared my desk from that goldfish bowl I made a promise to myself. I would never do another job that I disliked.

"Life is too short." I told myself. "Live it."

And so, that's exactly what I did...

2
FROM THE
FIRST NIGHT ON

They say you never forget your first time.

I've never forgotten my first night dancing.

It was a Saturday night. The train journey to London took longer than usual due to engineering works. I was late for my first shift.

When I finally made it there, I applied my makeup and put on my long black halter neck dress. It was compulsory to wear a long dress at the start of the shift and after midnight each dancer could change into a short dress, lingerie or a sexy uniform. I still have that dress;

I just can't part with it. I put on clear high heels, which most of the dancers wore. The heels were six inches high and the platform at the front was a couple of inches. To get used to wearing them I'd worn them round the house while cleaning. Not exactly homely attire, but I needed the practice. A lot of the girls called them slut shoes. Wearing them transformed our personas; we walked differently and carried ourselves more confidently – our backs straight, shoulders upright and chests out.

"Are you nearly ready?" The manager came to check on me in the dressing room.

I nodded.

"Stage name?"

"Tia" I said.

"Somebody else here already has that name, we can't have two girls with the same name, or it gets confusing with the pole rota."

I wanted Tia because Tia Maria was my favourite drink and I thought I would remember it easily. Now I had to come up with another name and fast, as the manager wanted to hand the rota to the

DJ. There was a poster on the back of the door advertising something for Christmas. There was a wreath on the poster.

"Holly? Do you have a Holly?"

"We don't, Holly will do just fine."

I made my way to the main floor of the club. There was an earlier shift for a private birthday party still in session, with topless ladies aplenty, dancing one to one with the rowdy men and one girl on stage against the pole. The venue looked and felt different to how it did on a teaching day, partly due to both genders being in the room. This was it. I was really here. A few of us "students" amalgamated, wracked with nerves. We knew we had to talk to customers to get a lap dance and earn our money, but we found it hard to pluck up the courage to approach them.

"Dancer etiquette" covers a number of rules; one being that if a dancer is already speaking to a customer, you *do not* interrupt. Another is the "five track rule." You may sit with a customer for five songs and if by then he does not want a dance, you must leave and give another dancer a chance; unless he is paying for a "sit down."

From The First Night On

A "sit down" is when a customer pays you a set fee per hour or half hour to sit with him. This may include drinking champagne, chatting and lap dances. I couldn't believe that this was "a thing," but some customers would just want the company of one girl they'd take a shine to. Some would have more than one girl at a time, or after their sit down with one, they may book a different girl.

Some of the new girls were already getting sit downs; looking like they were very engaged in their conversations, chatting away to their customers, nodding in agreement, drinking and smoking (back in the day before the smoking ban). I was having trouble approaching a customer to even say hello. Finally, a dancer roused from her seat and there was a space for me to approach one. I sat next to him, asked his name and struck up a conversation.

"Surely I'm saying the same things the other girls are?" I thought, "Surely this man is bored of the same chatter?"

Nevertheless, I continued, until I found such a time to ask if he wanted a dance, to which he replied:

"No, I'm okay right now thank you."

I was stumped. What could be said after that? Absolutely nothing. I had been knocked back. He was supposed to say yes! Time to move on. I left him and went and stood with another dancer. It was her first night too after completing the same course I'd attended.

"Any luck?" she said

"Nope" I said, disheartened. I felt like I was at a school prom with no partner and just sitting at the sidelines of the dance hall.

Approaching guys before another dancer reached them was also difficult. I had images in my head of rugby tackling girls to the ground or trampling over them in my six-inch heels to reach the victory point – the customer. I smiled to myself shamefully for thinking such a thing, but I couldn't help it. I was so desperate to do well, but hadn't realised how competitive it would be. I expected men to be on a conveyor belt, wanting one girl after another and throwing money at me. Alas that was not the case. This job was to involve hard work, like any other. As the hours rolled and the "no thank yous" continued, I became progressively more agitated, which probably made the situation worse. One thing you learn in this job is if you are in a bad mood, men can sense it and it hinders you from getting a dance.

2am came. One hour to go and so far, not one dance. Thank goodness I brought my house fee with me to pay up front. A house fee is the amount of money you pay the venue to work, regardless of whether you make money. Prices vary from venue to venue. Years before I started dancing, with "striptease shows", girls *did* get paid a wage. Now, in venues with private dances, you're more like a market trader paying for a pitch.

Within the last hour, two new customers entered and sat down. After they received their drinks from the waitress (another rule – you had to always wait until they had their drinks delivered to them), I made my way over with another girl. By this time, I had no expectations for any dances. I sat in the tub chair beside one of the gentlemen. They were from Switzerland but spoke fairly good English. I explained it was my first night and he asked how I was finding it. We had been taught never to say work was bad, or that we weren't earning, so I simply said:

"For my first night, it's going okay."

I asked questions like how long was he in England, and was he here for business or pleasure. He asked me where I was from and what job I did before I started this job. Three songs into the conversation, knowing I only had two left before I'd have to move on, I asked the burning question again:

"Would you like a dance?" He nodded.

I was so pleased I wanted to jump up and down and scream. Someone had said "yes" to me! I grinned with excitement. I stood up and moved forward to his seat. The song began, I started to move as I had been taught by the dancers in the course. My whole body was trembling with fear. This was my first tableside dance.

"Remember, remember, remember the moves," I kept telling myself. "Take off your dress, don't trip over it".

I hoped I didn't look too vacant for Mr. Swiss, but I seemed to have his undivided attention, so I must have been doing something right. The song ended, I leant forward and kissed him on the cheek and he said thank you. He complimented me and said I did well. I put my dress back on and he handed me ten pounds. I smiled, thanked him and walked away. My first private dance. There was no going back; I was officially a tableside dancer. A wave of relief washed over me, despite the fact I had only done one dance. I had still done *a* dance and that was all that mattered. 3am came and it was time to take off the make up and put on my jeans.

My train wasn't until 5.30am so I had to sit around at a very cold Victoria station. I didn't get home until 7.30. It had been a terribly long day and I hadn't even covered my expenses, but I was too tired to care.

From The First Night On

I told myself that my second day at work could only get better, and I was right…

3
VARIED VENUES

As the weeks progressed, I found myself getting more confident asking for dances, but I had yet to tell my Granddad that I had become a dancer. As far as he knew I was still working at the solicitors' office. He drove past me one day when I was out in town (during my old office hours) and I hid behind a car so he wouldn't see me. I was unsure what his opinion would be of me changing career. I also wanted to make sure I was going to stick to the dancing permanently before I had that conversation with him.

I was nowhere near the top earner in the strip club, but I was making okay money. I finally had my first sit down, which felt strange and very awkward. The guy was American, middle aged and very happy to request a sit down, yet hardly spoke. I found it extremely difficult trying to think of things to say when the conversation was all one sided. It ended with him leaving after 30 minutes but I still had an hour's worth of money off him. I worked four nights per week and began avoiding weekends, as the club wasn't that busy Fridays and Saturdays. Businessmen liked to get back home to their families at reasonable times on Fridays, so Thursdays they could have a late one and pretend they were doing overtime at the office, making them our busiest nights.

A fellow dancer mentioned another West End club that offered fully nude dancing. The difference, other than not keeping your thong on, was that nude dances paid £20 instead of £10. I arranged to go in for a working audition, which meant doing a pole audition and working to test out the club the same night. Working auditions were more worthwhile for me, seeing as I didn't live in London and if I didn't want to go back there, at least I wouldn't be out of pocket.

The club was lit up inside with soft red lighting. The stage was larger than the one in Mayfair, and the girls in the dressing room seemed more approachable. Much like my very first topless dance, I trembled doing my first nude one. I was so nervous that as I was pulling my thong down to take off, it got stuck between my heel and the inner sole of my shoe – hardly a good start.

"Remember to pull the thong right over your shoes next time", I told myself.

I made more money the first night at this club than I had made in any night in Mayfair.

It was at this stage I decided to tell Granddad about my new profession. Although he was fitted with a hearing aid, the tinnitus that accompanied his Ménière's Disease meant the aid hardly worked, so talking slowly, clearly and loudly in his presence was often easier, with the accompaniment of a notepad and pen for words he had trouble picking up.

Whilst I was partly worried about telling him, Granddad had always been pretty open-minded. Being born in 1925 didn't mean he was demure. People today think that generation was prim and proper. It wasn't. We in this day and age didn't invent sexuality; it just wasn't spoken about as freely back then. I remember Granddad telling my friends at home after my 21st birthday party about how we should enjoy ourselves whilst we're young:

"I mean, during the war, I had sex for half a biscuit in Hong Kong."

Varied Venues

I nearly dropped the kettle as I was making the tea when I heard him say that.

I felt a little tense, as no one necessarily wants their grandchild to be looked upon as a sexual object.

> "I've got something to tell you Granddad. I'm not working at the solicitors anymore, they fired me."

> "What are you doing now then?" he asked, concerned.

> "I don't want you to be worried," I said slowly, "I started it a few weeks ago. I'm working in a club, stripping and dancing."

He frowned.
> "You're WHAT!?" I raised my hand up to calm the situation.

> "Granddad it's perfectly safe, I work up in London, there are lots of rules and the club looks after us. Men aren't allowed to touch us; they get kicked out if they do. There are bouncers all the time around us and I make good money."

I told him how much I made some nights. His frown softened and he raised his eyebrows:

"Well that's not all bad then babby."

Once he knew I was safe and earning good money, I had won him over.

Three nights per week (this club was only open Tuesdays, Wednesdays and Thursdays), I stayed in London hotels. The difference was immense: it meant I got to bed earlier and relaxed all day and I was earning enough money to live that lifestyle.

Famous people came into this club: actors, footballers, and singers with their entourages. A lot of the dancers were real party girls, so if the club decided to continue their evening after hours, which was more often than not, the girls would stay behind to drink more. I always left at 3am and other than going to a late-night restaurant sometimes, would go immediately to bed. This meant that I was one of the only level-headed girls the following night. The majority were still usually hungover and so took a while to get "in the zone", while I was already making money.

I was really enjoying being a dancer. So much so, that I decided to look for local work either side of my nights in London.

I'd heard of a company that had dancing nights every weekend in two of their clubs. This was slightly different - table dancing once a month in Essex and lap dancing every Saturday in Kent and Essex. The table dancing night included a meal for the gentlemen whilst they listened to a comedian, following which their tables would be cleared, then the comedian would introduce the girls who would then dance *on* the tables. Once again, this company said I could do a working audition.

The two changing rooms there were heaving with 70 girls. Where I was used to wearing a long dress as work attire, girls here were wearing thong bikinis, or short, tight dresses and boots or high heels.

I smiled at a couple of girls but they were quite evasive, so I left them to it. Madison, Jenna and Claire said hello to me and I introduced myself. Claire was 18 and it was her second night there, Jenna had got her the job as she was dating one of Jenna's relatives and wasn't earning enough money cleaning houses for a living. Madison had just had breast enlargements and it was her first night back in a couple of months. She was stunning; tall, with DD boobs, an hourglass figure and beautiful, long, blonde curly hair. I was mesmerised. Madison was officially my first girl crush. The three seemed awkward around me.

"How old are you?" asked Jenna

"I'm 25." I replied.

It turned out the reason for them feeling uncomfortable was because they thought I was under 18.

"I'll take that as a compliment," I laughed.

We all had to stand backstage behind the curtains until our names were called to make our grand entrances. I peered through – there were so many men it made me nervous.

"How many guys do you think are out there?" I asked the girl standing next to me.

"Oh, about 300 or so." she casually answered.

I don't even recall 100 men in one night coming through the door in London, but here they'd all arrived before us. It was rowdy; men were banging on the tables, cheering for the girls to come out. One by one, we lined up across the stage. The room was full of smoke and reeked of beer. Once we were all called out, the comedian finished on the microphone with:

"Off you go girls!"

And like horses bolting they all jumped off the stage and onto tables, or ran off to the tables farthest away.

Varied Venues

I stood like a rabbit in headlights. I didn't understand what was going on as it was all very different from the clubs in London. I couldn't get a table so I stood around just observing. Girls were taking £10 notes off each table they were on and then the DJ played a song and they all danced. Well – as best as they could on tables. Girls stripped, crawled on all fours, laid on their backs and opened their legs wide for the men to see everything in between. Jenna was very petite, and she would do pull-ups on the light rigging whilst doing the splits in the air and the men cheered. When the song finished, the whole house applauded, the girls jumped down and ran to another table, still getting dressed whilst they ran along to save time, ready to collect another £10 for their next dance. The girls were on a mission. They took no prisoners and I was still unable to find a vacant table. I noticed two girls on one table together. One was standing up bent over and the other was leaning forward and burying her tongue inside of her. This was all too much for me. I'd gone from dancing in West End clubs with a one to three foot distance rule, to this. I felt out of my depth. I ran backstage to get my stuff and tried to open the fire exit to get out (with my bikini and heels still on) but I was unable to open it. I couldn't escape. One of the girls rushed backstage to get her lipstick, and knowing I was new, shouted down the corridor to me:

"Come on, there's money to be made!"

I couldn't leave without making a scene, so I put my bag down and went back out there. I found a table without a dancer and took the money and crawled on. It's only once I began my dance I understood why most of the girls stayed on their hands and knees or on their backs; the tables were so unstable it was safer that way. The faded red tablecloths were sodden with beer and covered my skin as I moved up and down along the trestle, whilst cigarette ash that had dropped onto the cloth left grey patches all over my body. Five guys either side of the table meant they were all pretty close to me and I had to keep my wits about me; watching their hands, heads and mouths to avoid them getting too close. It's amazing how men, after they've had a few drinks in that environment, suddenly believe themselves to be back street gynaecologists.

I continued from one table to another, although not every one wanted me, so I also did lap dances in the booths at the sides of the room. I stuck to the no-contact rule I was used to in London, whereas all the other girls sat on guys' laps and continued grinding, which of course, is what "lap dancing" is – dancing *in* their lap. The night dragged and I made £100, whereas the other girls had much more to count out. I had now experienced the dancing scene out of the West End and although it was a shocking and complete contrast, I decided to stick it out and go back the following month to table dance again.

Varied Venues

The next time I was ready to spring onto a table and ready to grab someone for a private dance. It was all about being feisty at this venue, rather than the sophisticated, delicate temptress I was in London; although in Essex when the other girls were asking for dances, men would on occasion point over to me and say:

"We want the posh one,"

So thenceforth I was known as "the posh one" there.

****

Claire, Madison and Jenna became my main friends from this venue and I'd often spend time with Claire outside of work, hanging out at either of our homes.

I always drove to work in Essex, and one time Madison suggested I travel up to the club with them and split the petrol money, as they had a driver.

"He'll come and pick you up first as you're nearer to him, his name's Rick. It'd be nice for you to be able to have a drink with us at work for once."

Rick was polite and, I thought, cute, with auburn hair. Madison lived about a 10 minute drive along the road so he and I chatted in the car. Although he'd driven Madison, Claire and Jenna countless times, he had never seen me dancing at the club. So I explained how long I'd danced there for, and where else I worked. He lived in the same town I'd grown up in.

"What school did you go to?" He asked

"I went to the Grammar School from age 13."

"Which high school did you go to prior to that?"

I told him.

"And how old are you?" he pried.

"25. I'll be 26 in October."

He started laughing:

"You don't remember me, do you?"

"No, should I?" I frowned

"I used to go out with you."

And then he gave me his full name. He didn't twig it was me to start with because he was told to pick up "Holly."

I was speechless. Sure enough, he was the guy I'd dated in high school; I was a librarian there, he'd borrowed a book and I'd stamped it. That's pretty much how we met. He was much shorter then so time had been good to him as he'd shot up way beyond me, and had also got much better looking. And he was my first ever 'proper' kiss, which happened at the school disco.

Fate had brought us together as friends again and we still talk to this day. I've had and will always have a soft spot for Rick. Many times he and I have supported one another through some tough times. And many have said we should have ended up together. But for some reason, we never have. And as I write this, I can honestly say I have never lost the attraction for him. But usually neither of us are single at the same time. And sometimes yes, I do daydream and wonder:

"What would my life be like if he'd been *the one*?"

****

Back at the club, not all the men were as well behaved as in London and the security weren't as strict either. For one, guys could go to the bar and not remain seated for table service, unlike in Mayfair. I lap danced for a guy who seemed quite nice and polite and once I said my thank you (which is traditional after dancing for a guy, dumb really, if you think about it – "yes thank you for letting me grind on you Sir!"), I went to put my clothes back on but couldn't find my thong. I looked both sides of the armchair he was sitting in; not there…on the carpet; nada. Finally I looked at the guy and he was being really quiet with a funny look on his face. He'd put the thong in his mouth when I wasn't looking and then pulled it out, laughing his head off. As if I was going to put them back on after they were soddened from his saliva. Gross idiot. Luckily, I always brought a spare in my bag.

From that night on, I wrapped my thong around my wrist. That way I'd never risk losing it again. It's not unusual for men to try and steal dancers' clothes; I think they consider them trophies. They don't take into consideration that some of our clothes are custom made, or match another part of our outfit and can't easily be replaced. All they care about is adding to their stupid bloody stripper shrines.

That club was affiliated with a magazine for topless models, many of whom danced there, and they also sent dancers on tour – to dance one-off in a pub, night club, working men's club or whatever. They called this a Roadshow. They were nationwide. Some girls travelled to every one. I didn't attend any too far away because after travel time and fuel costs, oftentimes it wasn't cost-effective. I travelled to Wolverhampton once and only made £50 because the venue didn't promote the event so there was hardly anyone there. I didn't want to chance that again.

Because these were one-off events and there weren't many lap dancing clubs those days outside of London, the men didn't always know how to behave. I was on a table once at a Roadshow, on my hands and knees, butt in the air as I crawled along, when a man thought it would be really funny to try to pour red wine on my bum thinking it would just fall into and "fill up" my asshole. I think he'd been watching too many porn films of girls with gaping ani. Needless to say, I was not impressed and the men failed to understand why I was in a bad mood after – as if pouring wine into my ass was a regular favourite pastime of mine.

Work at the West end club started to die down during the football World Cup (men always put football before nude girls) and dancing in Essex just once a week wasn't enough, so I looked for more work in *The Stage* newspaper. An agency was advertising for dancers for pubs. They owned a pub in Shoreditch, East London, and others in and around London. Claire came with me to the audition, as she wanted more work too.

The pub was pretty small, dingy and hazy from cigarette smoke. Full of men in suits from the City and a few builders in their work clothes, Monday at 9pm was audition night. We got changed in a very small room behind the stage, where all the other girls' cases and bags were and didn't leave much room for us. As we came out, we watched girls who already worked there walk around with a pint glass to each man, who individually threw in a one pound coin. This "jug collection" paid for the show the girl was about to do. Regardless of how much or how little was in the glass, the girl still made the same effort. The customers loved audition night as it meant they could see a few shows without having to pay for them; regular girls hated audition night because it meant they would do fewer shows and most guys weren't interested in having a table dance when they could stare at free pussy on stage. Needless to say, Claire and I got the job.

Working a day shift there was a bit more difficult as there were fewer guys and the ones that were there were mostly coming in to see a specific girl they already favoured. These "regulars" were sometimes under the thumb of one dancer and woe betide them if they ever had a table dance off a different girl. Silly really, as the men had no say if their favourite girl had dances off other men; they just had to sit and wait.

Varied Venues

The table dances were akin to the Roadshow ones, although the tables were round and a bit smaller, with a pole in the middle so there was something more there for stability. Oftentimes it was a one-to-one table dance, rather than group dances I was used to, and the tables were higher up than the trestles, which meant we were further away from the customers. No chance of any wine accidents in Shoreditch. Because we were so high up, all customers could do was look *up* us – if you know what I mean. It was only when I danced for a customer who was a regular at the pub, but always chose different dancers, that I realised that's why most of the men had table dances here. I held onto the pole, moving around it, stripping off as I went along, bending over, crouching down, looking at him all the time, trying to be sexy without showing how much my knees were hurting whilst crouching down to reach near him in my six-inch heels. When the song was over, I said my usual thank you and added, like all dancers said in this bar:

"Was that ok?" Not expecting anything but a polite yes.

"Well not really."

I looked at him, confused, and tilted my head thinking I'd misheard and waited for him to say he was joking.

"I was rather hoping you'd open your pussy lips for me a bit more."

I was gobsmacked:

"Erm, s-s-sorry, w-what did you just say?"

"I was rather hoping you'd open your pussy lips up for me a bit more."

In this job, a lot of the time you have to be on the ball and be ready to have a smart arsed comment comeback.

"Oh. Well, sorry I didn't realise you wanted to see *all* that. Next time I'll get you a periscope" and I smiled sweetly.

He walked off sulking. He wouldn't ask for a dance off me again and it didn't concern me one bit. Despite being naked most of the time with this job, I liked to think I still held some sort of morality and could choose to do what *I* wanted without someone giving instructions what to do with my body for a measly £10. I was a stripper. From my blonde hair to my painted toenails and everything in between; I didn't realise I was supposed to donate my vagina to research on every shift. This place was awful and I wanted somewhere nicer to work.

Varied Venues

After seeing a TV show about a club in Soho called Sunset Strip I called for an audition and got the job. It was easy; the owners paid all dancers a small wage to do stage shows and in addition you could keep any tips men gave you – this time notes, not coins. I'd work a day shift or a middle shift so I could get my train home, and the money wasn't bad. Most of the time we'd just sit around in the changing room in our underwear chatting or reading, waiting for our next show, which was on average once an hour. In between going on stage we were allowed to go out, take a walk, go get lunch, do anything really, as long as we were back in time for our shows.

It was really relaxed and refreshing. We didn't have to mix with the gents in the bar if we didn't feel like it, although chatting sometimes encouraged them to come and watch our stage shows and tip us later. The wide entrance opened out onto the street, with a maroon awning and a red carpet that welcomed men in and made them feel like Lords. The bar was on the entrance level and stairs led down to the small auditorium. Red chairs in a semi circle faced the stage, which had two vertical poles and one horizontal pole, which some girls that were brave enough would hang off like trapeze artistes. To the left of the seating was a DJ booth, just big enough for two people and the CD stereo. Adjacent to the booth was the stage entrance. We would buzz the DJ via an intercom from the changing room, to let him or her know what music we wanted to dance to and we would buzz one more time once at the bottom of the stairs to let them know we were ready to start our show. I missed my footing once in my heels going down those stairs and fell – only a few steps, but I was wearing a bunny girl outfit so by the time I'd fallen I looked a bit sorry for myself with my ears all skew-whiff. An injured rabbit, but not quite roadkill. I had five minutes to gather myself whilst the DJ explained my lateness to the audience, who actually felt sorry for me and tipped me quite well. Sympathy dances can be just as lucrative.

There were some great characters in that bar, most of them older. One guy tipped if you danced to Madonna. He tipped me at my audition as I'd chosen one of her songs. Another would only tip if you wore stockings and suspenders, not just hold ups, because:

> "The pussy is considered the painting and the stockings and suspender belt is the frame to it."

Some other guys would tip with posh cakes, biscuits or a packet of stockings instead of money. A few girls wouldn't take the gifts as they said stockings wouldn't pay their rent and although I would have preferred cash from them, their gifts were still something I could use, wear or eat, so I accepted them. The cake the customer would always buy for me from a well-known patisserie round the corner never made it home; I gave it to the homeless girl at Tottenham Court Road tube station.

Varied Venues

Then there were those who didn't tip: "The Tramp" who sat in the club all day, holding a train ticket in his hand, waiting for new girls to go near him thinking he was holding money and then laughing at them when he saw the disappointment in their faces. He never tipped anyone. We hated him.

Sometimes we'd do shows where the atmosphere was so flat, we may as well have been dancing to an empty room. No enthusiasm, no applause, not one smile. Those were the days we had to entertain ourselves. We knew the guys who were the "pussy watchers"; the ones who *only* looked in *that* area. They'd follow it everywhere with their eyes and even turn their heads. For my own amusement, when these guys were in, I'd literally sidestep from one pole to the other and back again, going faster and faster and chuckling to myself as they resembled spectators at a game of tennis following the ball. The funniest thing was they never realised what we were doing because they were so fixated. Our pussies had power: hypno-pussies.

I loved working at the Sunset, not just because I got paid a wage instead of paying a house fee, but also because I actually got to perform *proper* stage shows, with little costumes and I themed my music to the costumes, just like in the movies I'd watched. But I still wanted more work. The next step was modelling…

4
EYES, TEETH AND TITS

he Essex club that was affiliated with the topless magazine
gave me my foot in the door for modelling. I went out with
Madison and Jenna to a couple of "Models' parties" in London and
the club had some photographers from the magazine snapping girls
throughout the night. I watched and learned from my two friends
and then just copied what they were doing. The parties were usually
on a Friday and so if we made it into the magazines we would be
published in the next release the following Sunday. We ended up
being the centre of attention on those nights out. We'd play up to the
cameras, always getting our boobs out, licking each other's nipples,
straddling one another. Looking like typical good time girls. But
perhaps the craziest moment was when we came out of the club.

Nothing prepared me for what I was about to experience. I mean, I'd seen celebrities on TV getting "papped" coming out of clubs. But I never expected myself to be one of those people.

Walking out of the nightclub, there were paparazzi outside. At least 10 of them, all snapping photos and with lights so bright I didn't know where I was looking. I just posed as best I could, with Jenna and Madison, in our short skirts or tight trousers and with our tits out of our tops. Smile, look sultry, look cheeky, lick a nipple, stick your chest out, push your butt out – basically change the expression and movement with every pose. And then tell them your name so they would get it right if the pictures went to print. After a few photos our driver shouted for us to hurry up and we walked to where the car was parked; only a walk ended up turning into a run in our slut shoes as the paparazzi followed us with their cameras. They wouldn't give up. They sped up alongside us, still trying to take photos, so we'd stop, pose for one, thinking that would be enough and then continue on and they would speed up again. We finally reached our car and they laid across the bonnet, taking photos through the windscreen; our driver had a few choice words at them:

"Get off my fucking car!"

It was insane. I was a nobody yet there I was, running away from paparazzi like an A-list celebrity. They literally went mad for tits.

Did I like it? Being chased as if I was a celebrity? At the time, yes I did. I was buzzing. I'd never experienced anything like that before and I could understand why Jenna and Madison did a lot of modelling. It made me feel good and important. On Sunday I was in the paper; a photo of Jenna licking my nipple. That was my first picture. My Granddad, aunts and uncles weren't impressed. It wasn't exactly the perfect photo they could put on their mantelpieces. As the weeks went on, more photos appeared, from in the club and outside on the way to the car. People I danced for began to say they'd seen me in the papers and magazines. The only thing was I hadn't been paid for those photos. So there were plenty of topless photos of me and I hadn't seen a penny of what the paparazzi had been paid.

"If you want to get paid" said Madison "Then you'll need to sell a story. We do it all the time. We're *kiss and tell* girls. I'll introduce you to Nina at the next party. She works for one of the papers and works on the stories we give her."

When I met Nina the following week she was surrounded by models, taking it in turns to chat to her about what she could write about. She was really polite and friendly to me.

"So you want to be in the paper a bit more do you?" She asked.

I nodded.

"Ok, well have you slept with anyone famous?"

I shook my head. To be honest if I had, I don't think I would have told her. The last thing I wanted to do was tell the nation who I was having sex with.

"Do you lap dance?"

"Yes I do. On the Roadshows and in London."

"Well if you've danced for anyone famous, we can do something on that."

I explained to her that I had danced for a footballer, but other than that I had seen other celebrities in the club in the West End but I hadn't danced for them myself.

"That's okay, we can say you did. We always bend the truth." She smiled. "We'll   start with the footballer story first as he plays for the Premiership. We can sort you out a photoshoot in London that you'll get paid for and you'll also get paid for each story once they're published. You just have to send us an invoice when it's out. The story will feature your photo next to it."

After the weekend I rang Nina and told her the ins and outs of the lap dance I gave the footballer, not that there was much to tell, and then she put her own slant on it. Two weeks later I was in the paper, topless, with a whole page on how I danced for him and he tried to hurry me up because he couldn't wait to see me with my clothes off. He may have been a Premiership footballer, but he hardly played apparently as he was injured (I'm going by what my football fanatic friends told me, I never actually followed any football team or game).

I saw these stories as harmless at the time, even when the stories weren't all true. The newspaper was aimed at men mainly, and I'm pretty sure they didn't actually care who I danced for; surely all they ever did was look at the pictures.

I think I earned £250 for the photoshoot, and then anything between £120 and £250 for a write-up, depending on the celeb and how much of a story there was. But I know that kiss and tell girls for other papers would sometimes get thousands, and without topless pictures; but for that they would have had to have slept or lap danced with someone of a pretty high status. Back then, the papers had money to buy stories. I liked being in the paper. I wanted to model and that was a sure-fire way of getting me there.

I sold several stories over a good few years. One friend of mine managed to sell a lot more by buying a celebrity gossip magazine, checking out where the famous people had been spotted around London, and then calling the paper and saying she's been wherever with a particular celebrity, and flashed her boobs. Clever – using second-hand evidence to gain some easy money.

I joined a couple of model agencies that looked for models and the more you said you'd take off, the more jobs you'd be put forward for. But I only wanted to do topless, or "art/classic nude", so I was willing to wait for the work.

Art/classic nude is also known as "tasteful nude," basically it's not graphic, i.e., you don't have any photos with your legs open (unless something is covering that area, like a prop or your hand). Then there was "English open leg/ UK Mag", whereby you model nude with your legs open, then "American/American open leg" where you do the same but it's more graphic – you hold your pussy lips apart so everyone can see in detail your genitalia. "Continental" was modelling with insertion of toys or fingers. Then there's XXX which is porn, so "Girl-girl" (GG), "Boy-Girl" (BG) and so on. Oh and

"Anal", "DP" (double penetration), the list goes on; there was always a "tick box" section whenever you registered with an agency.

A lot of choices, but imagine the company not asking for as many boxes to be ticked, and then sending a girl to a shoot where they just assumed they would work up to a certain strength. It could create a wasted shoot day for a company and therefore no money for the model and no percentage to the agency. Ticking or not ticking boxes saved a hell of a lot of time for everyone. The girls at the club in Essex worked up to various levels; the ones who did just topless usually had big boobs, the majority being fake boobs – there weren't many naturally larger-busted girls with slender figures. Those in that minority, however, did get a lot of work due to it being unusual. Girls of all shapes and sizes did the higher-level work for films or print publications; the requirements weren't as specific.

There were times when photographers would make out you were booked for a harder level than you were, thinking you'd just agree to what they'd told you. One of my first modelling experiences outside of the newspaper shoots involved going to a photographer who had a studio local to me at his house. The booking was for art nude, yet plenty of times he tried to take sneaky pictures, saying:

"Could you just bend over a bit more…yes that's right, now if you could just move that leg a bit further apart…"

I stood up straight and sternly said:

"I've *told you*, I'm only doing art nude, *not* UK Mag."

He sulked and continued to take the photos that he didn't want to take. Photographers pushed harder with new models, thinking they wouldn't know the difference. We had to stand our ground and not get into anything we didn't want to do. Another thing photographers should not under any circumstances do, was to touch the model, but some would try anything for a bit of contact:

"Oh, your bra strap /stocking isn't quite right/ let me just move your leg to where it should be…"

Again, it was down to us to tell them we didn't feel comfortable with that, or they would keep on trying. Models would always talk and if a photographer ended up being too creepy or there were other warning signs, word soon got around. The majority of photographers were pretty good, but a few always tried to break the rules.

Because I limited my modelling levels, I continued to dance as my main source of income. The odd modelling job here and there kept my work varied and added to my pay packet. I enjoyed both and my timetable was pretty busy. Life was good and I was happy. I was learning more from the girls I worked with, with regard to how to look good/better and what looked good on me. I learned about sunbeds, the best fake tan to use, false nails, how to use liquid eyeliner and what hairpieces to buy to make my hair look fuller or longer.. Most men were buying into the fantasy of what they didn't have at home. And I liked that. Going back to dreaming of being a stripper when I was a child - with my admiration of the big hair, the glossy glamourous looks and sexy underwear - I was finally living that dream. I was turning into the women I'd admired.

Unfortunately not all my friends outside of dancing understood. They'd initially been supportive, but one night at our local pub the vibe I'd felt for a month or so was still lurking. Someone complimented me on my nail colour. Immediately my friend Jamie butted in and said:

"Well, her nails are *fake*."

I ignored the comment and we carried on our conversation. A few minutes later another mutual friend came over to our group to say hi. I hadn't seen many people in my hometown for a while so they were inquisitive as to what I was up to and how my new career was going. The mutual friend asked if I'd been on holiday as I was looking a little darker compared to my usual skin tone of Casper the

Friendly Ghost white. I was about to say no, I'd had a couple of sunbeds, but again Jamie interrupted with:

"It's *fake*"

She started to get my back up. I never pretended that anything was "real", yet she always felt the need to try and put down whatever I was attempting to do to make myself feel better or improve my appearance. I wasn't the only one who noticed. My other friends intervened:

"Well your skin tone has a nice healthy colour"

or:

"Where do you get your nails done because I'd like to come with you?"

And bless them for trying to keep the peace between Jamie and I, as well as showing me their support. Needless to say the friendship with Jamie rapidly dissolved. I never felt distant from the group again. It had just been Jamie giving off that vibe. I'd always had issues with the way I looked and didn't need anybody, let alone someone I considered to be a friend, putting me down. It was bad enough at work some days with customers criticising one thing or another because something "wasn't quite right". I certainly wasn't going to listen to it from someone I was beginning to believe was either jealous of the compliments I was receiving, or had her own self esteem issues. Nobody deserves that. I started to see why a lot of dancers and models just hung out with their own kind. We understood each other. We never judged, we just encouraged. We were cut from the same cloth, no matter what walk of life we were from. And I loved that. I trusted the small clique of girls I worked with. We were close.

5
WHAT HAPPENS IN DRESSING ROOM , STAYS IN THE DRESSING ROOM

I walked into the dressing room, found a workspace to get ready and placed my case on the counter. We all had small travel cases. For a while if you ever saw a girl on public transport in London with a travel case on wheels, with a certain look about her, you could tell she was in the industry - you *just knew*. You'd think we wouldn't need any more than a rucksack or small bag with the skimpy clothes we wore, but add to our itinerary make up, hair brushes and styling products (and sometimes a drier, tongs or straighteners), shoes, baby wipes, our choice of music on CD and for some venues, 6 or 7 outfit changes, then a bag on wheels was the most convenient way to carry it all from A to B; sometimes quite a long way.

We always stripped down to our underwear before doing our makeup and hair so marks from the lines of the clothing we'd travelled in had time to fade. I generally either sat on a small towel or my coat so the chair wasn't too cold on my bum wearing just a G-string.

The dressing room had a counter running round the perimeter, with about 5 feet in between to walk around. Bright white bulbs surrounded the mirrors and lit up like in the Hollywood films. The lights weren't flattering; they didn't need to be. They did their job of highlighting every flaw we had so we could apply concealer to the pimple that had just popped up, or pluck out the stray eyebrow hair that was growing in the wrong direction. We were aiming for perfection in the bright room, so we would look even better in the dimly lit room downstairs where we worked.

I'd applied my concealer and foundation and was about to work on my smoky eye look with my eye shadow palette, when an American girl called Emma who was sitting at the counter behind me on the other side asked:

"Does anyone have a spare hair tie?"

"I might have, let me check" I said.

"Oh thanks, I've not met you before, I'm Emma."

"Holly, I've been here for a month; nice to meet you."

I stood up to look in my case and rummage for the hair tie. Bending over, whilst I looked, Emma added:

"You have a really nice butt by the way."

Girls always complimented each other in the dressing room. It was liberating to receive them as well as give them out, seeing the good in each other, unlike my ill-fated friendship with Jamie. We were all in competition with regard to earning money, but in another way we were a team. I smiled:

"Thanks!" I'm sorry I don't seem to have a spare one, but you can use the one I'm using."

"Oh no, don't be silly, you need it."

"Honestly it's fine, I've put my foundation on already so my hair won't be in the way if I take it down and do the rest of my makeup."

Her green eyes lit up with gratitude as I leaned over to give it to her.

We all finished getting ready and continued with general idle chit chat: men, money and customers.

I put on my short black Lycra skirt, black padded bra, a pair of sheer lace top hold-ups and my 6-inch heels and then finished off blow drying my hair. Emma walked back over with the hair tie:

"Here, let me finish your hair for you,"

She could see I was struggling with getting the back to curl under. A couple of the girls had left to go downstairs as the club was going to open in a few minutes.

"I don't want you to be late on the floor because of me" I said, worriedly.

"I've been here for years, don't worry, you won't get me in trouble. Plus as long as they have a couple of girls downstairs they're not particularly bothered about everyone being down there at once."

She finished my hair in no time. I stood up to pack away everything back in my case and she remained next to me.

"Oh, your stockings aren't level."

I turned to face the mirror with my back to it

"Ah dammit, I *always* do that! So frustrating!"

"Here, let me do it."

She crouched down behind me and adjusted the one on my right leg,

"There, that's much better."

I turned back to look in the mirror to check:

"Ah, thanks again Emma! You've done my hair *and* dressed me today" I said jokingly.

As she stood up, she moved closer to me and put her hand on the back of my hair.

"You're welcome."

She moved closer and kissed me on the lips, gently. Her lips felt so soft. She looked me in the eyes to get a response and I kissed her back. The other girls didn't say a word, carried on about their business and went downstairs. I'd wondered if she'd done this before? She must have. She moved her mouth down my neck, breathing slowly, giving me goose bumps, and finally reaching my boobs. She didn't take my bra off, just pulled one of the cups down and started to kiss, lick and suck my nipple, whilst squeezing the other boob over the top of my bra. I forgot I was at work, ignored the ugly bright lights illuminating us and let Emma do whatever she wanted. I stroked the back of her neck lightly with my nails and her hand moved to the top of my thigh. She ran it from the lace of my hold ups, up into my skirt to feel the heat coming from inside my G-string. I stepped back to sit on the counter and she cupped the palm of her hand over the front of my pubic bone and just held her fingers in between my legs. My eyes widened, waiting for her to move her hand and touch me more intensely and I wriggled, to entice her to do more to me.

She looked at my face and whispered:

"Have you ever done this before at work?"

"No" I giggled.

"Well, this happens a lot, but when you're a new girl, no one really tells you about it until you've settled in so you don't get the shock of your life."

Heather walked back into the dressing room.

"Up to your old tricks again Emma?" she said smiling, whilst Emma still had her hand up my skirt.

Heather kissed her in front of me with her darkly glossed lips. It was a real turn-on to see and I leant towards them, taking it in turns to kiss them both on the neck, whilst they tongued each other.

Heather pushed me back against the mirror and started to suck on my tits just like Emma had before she walked in on us. Emma moved my G-string to the side to make room for her fingers. I was so wet, turned on with the anticipation of what was happening. I hadn't had a woman before, let alone two at the same time, but something told me I was about to get the ride of my life…

…and if you believe that this is really what happens in a strip club changing room, then you'll believe anything.

6
WHAT REALLY GOES ON BACKSTAGE

If you were taken in by that little story, thinking it was the truth until I set you straight, you wouldn't be the first. Most of the men I talk to actually think that dancers are all having it away with each other backstage and that it's some sort of free-for-all lesbian gang bang. I think those men have been watching too many glossy porno movies. If they believe that's real, they probably also believe the big burly plumber always gets his end away when he goes to fix a housewife's washing machine talking in a German accent.

I did get my pussy licked once, for a couple of minutes in one of the bathrooms, but I won't bore you with the details. You probably now already have images of that conjured up in your head, and that's enough for your mind to go off on a tangent.

Usually the most erotic looking thing you'd see in a dressing room is one girl rubbing fake tan into another girl's back. The reality of it, and most managers and DJs will more or less tell you the same, is that the majority of strippers/exotic dancers or whatever you want to call us, are hogs. The condition of some of the dressing rooms I have been in is truly disgusting and it amazes me women don't care how they leave their workstations/dressing areas. Girls who brush their hair and empty their brushes on the floor because they can't be bothered to walk over to the bin. Baby wipes all over the floor because they missed the bin or because the toilet bin is overflowing with shitty/bloody baby wipes (yes, believe me). Gum stuck under the workstations. Spilled drinks where they can't be bothered to mop them up. Piss all over the seats where some girls stand – yes *stand* – on the toilet seats and piss on them. When we were backstage on a Roadshow, waiting to be called out one by one, our manager wouldn't let a girl go to the toilet as it meant she'd have to go out on the floor past the men and ruin the introduction. So she pissed in a pint glass. That same girl apparently shat in one at another Roadshow (although that could just be hearsay). I'll give her her dues; she must have had a good aim. I'm not that talented. I also have issues with going to the toilet in front of people. If I didn't, it may have saved me from the time I got stuck in the toilet backstage at the Essex club because the lock broke. I had to wait until people walked past the door (it wasn't a cubicle in a main restroom, it was a room in an old building with just one toilet and a very solid door) and bang on it and yell out:

"Help! Can anyone hear me? I'm locked in!"

With the amount of girls at the club the main problem was someone hearing me over the loud chattering. Finally someone went and got the manager who shouted:

"Stand back Holly!"

I did, thankfully, as he karate kicked the door in (he was a martial arts instructor on his days off from organising strippers) and I walked out, grateful, but a little embarrassed.

In some of the pubs we had to make do with just a normal room to get changed in if it was a once-a-week venue, and they were usually a bit of a mess compared to the glamorous strip clubs, but either way, us girls shouldn't try to make the environment worse. Not that some pubs even cared about where we got changed. I've changed in two changing rooms where they've had cockroaches and no one seemed to bat an eyelid while in my head a voice was shouting:

"HELLO!? Cockroaches!? No pest control? Am I the ONLY one who's concerned here!?"

There was one pub which had actual dog shit on the carpet which was left there like it was a normal thing. Then there was the pub with the rat. I'm shuddering just thinking about what I've endured over the years. All of those experiences made you zip up your bags in the changing rooms to avoid taking any unwanted guests home.

Sometimes changing rooms can be "clinical". Leaning back on a table with your legs wide open and asking –

"Does that look like an ingrown hair to you?"

whilst three or four girls look close up at your genitalia to give second, third, fourth and even fifth opinions demonstrates how there is at times a level of trust with the ones we work with.

Then there are stripper fights, and not all of them are backstage. Some are heated arguments over using another girl's song, some are regarding "stealing" someone's customer, whilst others are over "dirty" dancers (doing more than they should) and the clean girls getting pissed at them. Some are simply due to paranoia from drug use. Some are one girl sticking up for another, or making up lies about another. It's usually always blown out of proportion. We could tell when a stripper fight was going to go down. The strippers ready to rumble would kick their heels off. We may be careless with regard to some things but never let it be said that we don't think about health and safety in a heated argument.

The rule in any venue was "watch your money, your phone and your clothes." I carried a small padlock for my stripper case. It's horrible to think that you are all there doing the same job, day in day out together, and yet at times there may be someone who wants to steal from you. I've even known girls to have their day clothes stolen so they've had to go home wearing stripper clothes. It's not always that their clothes are designer makes either; it's just out of spite. Perhaps the girl who had her clothes stolen earned better than the girl who stole. Jealousy prevails at times, unfortunately.

For sure, venues can get bitchy. Attitudes can run rife in venues with a large number of dancers. New girls can end up putting the regular girls' noses out of joint, which has resulted in vandalism of their dance outfits. I've heard one girl had her thigh boots slashed up with scissors by girls who didn't like her; but of course no one saw anything happen and no one would own up to it. Actions like that would usually push the new girls out as they wouldn't want to face more of their belongings being trashed, and who could blame them? Luckily, the worst I've had was a dress stolen (custom made, I hasten to add) by a so-called "friend." I never saw her wearing it as we never worked together after that shift, but several told me she had it as it was a dress that really stood out. The sad thing is that these are the "tools of our trade." My Granddad, ever wise, would say:

"You should never steal another workman's tools."

If only he'd given lectures on morality to strippers.

Managers and DJ's get idolised by customers in strip joints. Many a time have I heard words to the effect of:

"Ah mate, I envy you with all this tit, ass and pussy around you, you have the *best* job in the world!"

But the managers and DJs disagree. Try dealing with the fights, dramas, bitchiness and between 10 and 70 or so (depending on the size of the club) girls all PMS-ing at once because their menstrual cycles are synchronised.

But perhaps the funniest dressing room memory that still makes me laugh now – and my friends always get me to tell this story – is the night I was finishing a day shift at work and there were two girls getting ready on the shift change. They were, I think, Brazilian, talking to each other in their native tongue and looked up at me as I walked in. Because they didn't recognise me, they continued to chat amongst themselves and get on with getting ready. One of them was using an epilator to de-fuzz her legs. I was sitting by the workstation opposite them so on occasion couldn't help but look at them via the mirrors. Now I'm the type of person who can't stand awkward silences and especially with girls I don't know, I'll always try to make eye contact and smile, or polite conversation to at least break down barriers, and for girls to know I'm not standoffish, or to feel like I'm any threat to them. (Girls can be quite impersonal at times.) As I was putting on my clothes, I thought of a great ice breaker. I'd ask if the epilator was any good as I was used to waxing. So I turned around on my chair to talk to her. As I spun, the girl crouched down, ankles wide, and proceeded to shave her asshole. I'd already spent two seconds too long facing them both and couldn't swivel back or they'd think I had an attitude problem. So there I am, facing them, and I've committed to facing them, and they're looking at me, and I'm looking at them, and she's still shaving her ass hair:

'Erm,' I said, in a high-pitched tone, 'Are, are those things…any good?'

'Oh, fantastic!' She replied. 'Best invention ever!' (Still shaving away.)

I smiled, nodded and turned away to pick up my stuff. They carried on as if it hadn't happened, whilst I was completely dumbfounded. Taxi for one - Holly Burnett.

No two days were the same in the dressing room. It was out on the floor that things became mundane at times; namely the repetition of what each customer would say to us…

7

BLA , BLA , BLA

With every job comes monotony in one form or another. It's just the way it is.

I have never been a fan of monotony; that's probably why I disliked being in a goldfish bowl of an office prior to dancing. It's also plausibly why I functioned better as a dancer in different venues rather than just one. Different girls, different customers and different management. Whilst we'd meet a variety of people in venues, from the men in suits to the manual labourers, they were still all there for one thing: naked women.

BLA , BLA , BLA

The men in groups on a lads' night out for a celebration. The ones just killing time before heading off to watch a football game, or going to catch their train. The colleagues who had a long week and needed to unwind before going home. Lonely individuals who wanted the company of a lovely lady for a chat and a dance. And the ones who were so caught up in the fantasy that they were there to pick up a dancer who would be the woman of their dreams and end up being their girlfriend; whence they would drive off into the sunset and live happily ever after (whilst the dancer became their wife and wore nothing but her strip clothes and strip shoes, even at home, cleaning).

We always asked the same questions to spark up the conversation. We'd introduce ourselves, ask their names, where they're from and if they'd been to the venue before. Then the conversation could pretty much verge off in any direction dependent on how chatty the guy was. But oftentimes they would ask us the same inquisitive questions; or if we asked them questions related to asking them for a dance, excluding a straightforward yes or no, they more often than not ended up replying with the same answers dancers have been hearing for years. From the dawn of stripper time and beyond my retirement, it continues.

So I present the first part of this series – and it's probably easier to give it in list form. It's in no particular order and is obviously going to sound a little whingey as this is what got on our nerves at work. I like to call it:

<u>"If I had a pound for every time a customer said…"</u>

During jug collections:

Dancer asks for a pound, customer asks what it's for yet they've asked all the other girls before you and have been there long enough to know. Pointless stalling.

Dancer asks for a pound and the customer says:

"I don't have any change"

"It's ok, I have change, I can change a 5/10/20"

"No thank you"

It's as if whilst offering to help them you've insulted them by resolving a situation, or they don't trust you to give back all of their change. Ridiculous.

When you ask if they'd like a private dance, here are some of the replies:

"No thanks, I don't dance"

"What's a private dance?"

I reply:

"A lap dance"

"So what *is* a lap dance?"

"Well there are two key words here (moron): *lap, dance.*"

Not exactly rocket science is it?

"How good are you?"

Hang on, let me just get the folder of references out of my bag...

"I'm married."

Well you know what? I never asked to sleep with you, I asked if you wanted a dance. Besides, if you're really that worried about getting a lap dance, why are you here in a lap dance venue?

"Come back later," when in fact they mean "'Don't come back at all because I   don't want one."

Just be honest boys, it saves us time and we'd have more respect for you if you were honest and said no thank you.

"Why don't you give me some money and I'll dance for you?"

No.

"It's my birthday, is it free?"

No.

"Can you do me a dance for (£5/£10 less than the usual price)"

Absolutely fucking not.

"No thanks, I'm gay...and that's my boyfriend" (points to friend, he and friend laugh loudly thinking they're the first ones to ever crack that joke).

"To be honest, this really isn't my thing. I've only come in for a drink."

Go and drink somewhere else where there's no nudity then.

"This isn't really my thing. I'd rather take a girl out to get to know her."

Well this isn't speed-dating 101, so please go somewhere else. We're not here to date, we're here to *dance* – looking at girls naked, checking out the goods before you ask someone on a date is *not* the way forward!

"I've got a big cock."

What's your point? Oh hang on, did you mean to say you *are* a big cock? No? My mistake.

"I can't have a dance off you because you look like my sister/mum/aunt/wife."

Fair comment (if it's true).

"You make enough money doing this so I'm certainly not giving you any."

Believe me, I don't get paid enough to listen to your bullshit.

> "I don't want a dance but good luck to you; you're really gorgeous and sexy."

Aww thanks. Compliments pay my bills threefold.

> "Do you do extras?"

I'm out of gravy, but I do have chips or coleslaw, so what'll it be?

> "How much is a dance?"

> "£20"

> "What do I get for £40?" (winks)

> "Two dances" (winks back)

When conversing with customers with the aim to getting a dance, they are always curious to know more about us:

> "What's your name?"

> "Holly."

"No it's not."

"Okay, it's Margaret."

"You're not going to tell me, are you?"

"No."

"Where are you from?"

"I'm English"

"No you're not."

Whether we lie or not they never believe us anyway.

"What's your day job/what do you do in your normal life?"

"I'm a teacher" (their fantasy, for some reason, this usually works a treat to get dances).

Or to confuse them:

"I put the dots on dice/ I wash dolphins/ I put the holes in bourbon biscuits."

"How much money do you make?"

This is probably *the most* annoying question ever asked. I would never even ask my friends how much money they make, and I certainly would never pry to a stranger. When I've flipped the conversation back to them and asked them how much they earn, they look at me as if I'm really rude to ask, so why is it ok to ask any of us?

"This job must make you so horny/ do you get turned on when you do this?"

If anything, this job can do the opposite really. Listening constantly to guys talking to me like I'm a sex object, or talking to us about our body parts doesn't exactly do anything for us. We're not doing this job because we're sex-starved or sex-craving women. Customers are deluded.

"Do you parents know you do this?"

Do yours know you're visiting a strip club?

"Do you have a boyfriend?"

No.

"Do you want to go out sometime?"

No.

"Do you have a boyfriend?"

No.

"I bet it's hard to hold down a normal relationship."

"Do you have a boyfriend?"

Yes.

"What does he think of this?"

"If you were *my* girlfriend, I couldn't cope with you dancing for other men."

Well it's a good job I wouldn't date you in a million years then.

"Why do you do this to yourself? You're better than this."

Why do I work for a living, you mean, and support myself independently?

"You obviously have no respect for yourself."

It's not about lacking self-respect, it's about running a business. I get up and go to work every day, just like everybody else. The fact I do most of my work naked is neither here nor there.

"You don't belong here."

So where do I belong exactly? In an office? Tried that. Didn't like it.

"Let me take you away from all this."

And go where exactly? Your place? Or do you mean you're going to support me, pay my bills, shower me with gifts and let me be financially free? No? Didn't think so.

"What time do you finish?"

2am

BLA , BLA , BLA

"What are you doing after?"

Going home

"Can I come with you?"

Let me get back to you on that [avoids customer for the rest of the evening].

"What time do you finish?"

2am

"What are you doing after?"

Going to bed

"Well that's boring."

"So where's the after party?"

Although we didn't mind a night out, most men seemed to think we were all 24/7 party animals. But after wearing six inch heels on a seven hour shift, most of us just wanted to go home, remove our make up and go to bed.

The actual lap dancing could be a little monotonous too. We'd all pretty much stick to whatever routine we were comfortable with, as that way we'd work out how long our dance is and know it's timed properly (for the venues where you just started the dance at any point in a song). If you put two girls next to each other, they'd more than likely be dancing differently. Although I never found the routine tedious (unless I was doing more than two dances in a row for the same guy), I could guarantee there would, on almost every shift, be a customer who did at least one of these:

<u>Lap dancing habits</u>

Fidget in their chair. Either them gyrating underneath as I danced, moving their legs, moving their head and so on. Sit still for goodness sake!

Attempting to slap my ass when I bend over.

Attempting to lick a nipple when it's near them.

Trying to kiss or lick my neck or lick or blow in my ear, or *even* trying to blow on my genitalia. The worst thing that happened to me in this regard was with a very drunk man, and I admit I wasn't paying attention to him as I was looking over at three of my friends who had all finished dancing for one guy on his birthday. As I was bent over, I felt a tongue run up the back from my pussy to my ass area. I was still about two feet away from him, but he must have leant towards me. I jumped forward, spun round and just shouted at him. I can't even remember what it was I said now, but I was angry and disgusted. The three girls also ran over, realising what he'd done and so now the poor guy was sitting down, surrounded by four strippers, all shouting and standing over him. I can remember him being shit scared and repeatedly saying:

"I'm sorry, I'm sorry!"

The doorman threw him out.

Giving instructions on how to dance. For example:

"Oh yes, that's right, take your bra off".

It *will* all come off, but I will do it in my *own* time.

Try to touch, and when you tell them not to, ask:

"Not even a little bit?".

Obviously not.

Have no personal hygiene. Coming into a venue straight after work is one thing, as it's expected you may be a bit dirty if you work in construction, for instance; but men who have greasy hair, long fingernails, stained clothes and who smell on a normal day is totally different. Soap is *not* expensive.

Grunt/make animal type noises. It's so off-putting that you keep your distance in case they're about to blow their load in their trousers. You never can tell. A friend of mine made this mistake when she was kneeling down in between a customer's legs and rubbed her boobs against his crotch area. He got over excited and came, with no word of warning, making her boobs damp as it seeped through his clothes and somehow, she ended up with a rash on her chest.

Lick his lips/poke his tongue out when I'm dancing and happen to open my legs.

Try to touch my face. Do you have *any* idea how long it takes me to get my makeup right?!

Sniff. When you lean back or lean into them, they can't resist putting their nose near your neck or shoulders and inhaling really loudly through their nose.

If they get an erection when we're dancing, ask:

"Can you feel that?"

The majority of the time I'd say no just for kicks.

Hearing the same things, night after night, was of course mentally draining. The severe eyeball rolling moments that also led us to letting out deep sighs were pretty regular.

Some guys were verbally abusive assholes; those who were either insulting or generally had an attitude problem. Those were the men who were more than likely getting "hen pecked" at home, so would visit strip bars to try to exercise some type of authority to make them feel better. Once we knew who they were we'd avoid them most of the time so they'd end up leaving.

You'd be surprised how much we counsel customers; they'd pour their hearts out with their problems after a drink or two. The men who wanted to talk and talk and tell you that their wives didn't understand them.

The special requests:

"Can you dance barefoot? I like feet."

"Can you wear stockings/ Lace/ French knickers/ a thong?"

"Can I buy your old shoes/ your worn panties?"

You could never please everyone in one night; there was always someone wanting something different.

Work wasn't so awful I felt like I wanted to quit. I, like anyone else, would have liked to have done my job some nights with a little more ease. But no matter what job you do, there will always be a shitty day. All of these things happened over a 10-year stint. Not *everything* happened *every* day. If they did, I can safely say I probably would have quit!

> The Dealmakers, the serial Stripper Daters
> The Preachers and the Saviours
> The Misguided, the Divided
> The Curious and the Furious
> The Special Requesters, the Patience Testers
> The Propositioners, who were never Listeners
> The Misogynists, Philogynists
> And even the Gynaecologists

BLA , BLA , BLA

In one way or another, they all contributed to my income. And to this day, I thank every one of them.

8
SHIMMER

Granddad's eye became sore and he had a consistent headache. I took him to the doctor, who referred him to the eye hospital. By the time of his appointment, he looked like someone had punched him. It was red like a blood vessel had burst. The specialist suggested Granddad have his bloods done for erythrocyte sedimentation rate (ESR) and C-reactive protein (CRP). The following morning I had a call from the specialist (seeing as Granddad was particularly hard of hearing, the doctors always called me):

> "We have your Granddad's blood results back. They're both very high, so we'll need you to bring him in immediately for a biopsy."

Shimmer

Because I couldn't call Granddad to tell him not to eat or drink anything I jumped out of bed and drove over hastily. He was sitting down to drink a cup of tea and I walked into the living room and removed it from his hands. I spoke clearly and loudly and pointed to him, then to my eye and then said:

"Hospital, for an operation."

He was slightly flummoxed by me bounding in as I didn't give him much time to think or let it sink in, but even so I packed him a bag for the weekend; the operation was on a Friday and there wouldn't be any doctors until after the weekend to check his stats or discharge him.

They performed a Temporal Artery biopsy – where the surgeon took out a small part of the temporal artery, the major artery in the head, in order to get it checked out under a microscope where the lab techs would check for damage or inflammation (or both) of the lining. Granddad stayed awake during the procedure, a braver person than me I thought, although he didn't have much choice.

The results indicated he had Giant Cell Arteritis (or Temporal Arteritis), which, if left untreated, can cause blindness or a stroke (although we were never told that and we trusted the specialist). Treatment was a course of steroids and Granddad had to continue to see the eye specialist for checks, along with a rheumatologist to balance his drugs, seeing as he also had Meniere's Disease and Type 2 Diabetes. A rheumatologist was the best person to deal with this as an expert in inflammatory diseases of the blood vessels.

One minute the drugs prescribed would do their job, so we would drop the dosage of steroids down, very slowly as requested. Then suddenly it would flare back up like before, and Martin (my husband I was separated from, but still my best friend) and I would have to take him to A&E and he'd have to start back on the high dose and gradually dwindle it again. It was a game of chance. Granddad never felt 100% anymore and he was usually a quite active person for his age, forever doing carpentry up in his shed, making furniture, walking up and down all day unloading wood. But a combination of so many drugs and ailments left him either too tired or too down. Men from that era were always told to just pick themselves up. Even PTSD from the war was just "shell shock" and they dealt with it alone, or went to a mental hospital and stayed there (like Granddad's father, who had a metal plate put in his head during the First World War and was never right afterwards). So Granddad just sat in his armchair a lot, looking out at the world through the window, or watching the TV with subtitles. Doing the job I was doing was a godsend as I had all the time in the world to drive him to whichever check-ups he needed. It rarely interfered with my work.

****

Shimmer

Knowing I was great at organising, how dancing worked, and how venues operated, I decided to set up my own agency which I called *Shimmer Agency*. I had a plan. I was to set up a pole dancing "academy," train girls up and then offer them jobs. I knew I already knew a few girls, but some of those wouldn't necessarily work the jug pubs and some were too far away from where I wanted to initially focus – Kent, my home county. It made sense to target locally first.

I was renting a one bedroom flat, so Granddad let me make my old bedroom at his into a studio. I asked one of the workmen from the Shoreditch bar to supply and fit a pole, and then with batons on one side of the studio, I pinned black fabric to hang down off one half of the room's walls. Teaching from there meant that I was at Granddad's more and he'd have a bit more interaction when people arrived. Granddad always loved company.

Like the club had taught me when I went into the West End, I planned out my lessons, teaching pole tricks, lap dancing techniques and how to talk to customers. I taught how to dance to slow songs, faster songs (for some reason a lot of first timers always assumed they could only dance to slow and sensual rhythms, I showed them you could still be sensual with faster paced tunes too), and what to wear. I would teach one-to-one or up to four girls at a time. Some just wanted to learn pole dancing to make them feel sexier rather than to start a dancing career. I printed hand-outs for each of them, with photos of pole moves and lists of suggested outfits and songs to certain routines.

I was taking on a lot of responsibility, but I knew I could do it. I already had some girls on my books, so if work came up then I could use them initially and not worry about not having enough staff. The new girls were trickling in, so I knew I'd always have enough work.

To get the contracts for girls to work, I went through the phone directory and listed all the pubs in the area I wanted to cover. Then I printed out leaflets to either post or deliver to each pub, suggesting that they could potentially earn more money by having erotic dancers. Once I received a call from a venue, I arranged to go down and have a meeting with them. The idea was that I would charge half the house fee off the venue and half of the girls, but if the pub wouldn't pay then I'd get the girls to pay the full amount.

Some pubs wanted to do one-off nights, others went for regular monthly or weekly events. The first "contract" I had was Monday nights at a gay club. They never usually opened on a Monday so thought putting dancers in for the "hetero" community may work. Advertising wasn't easy. Most of the time I tried to give out flyers, guys would say:

"Oh, no that's a gay bar, I'm not going there."

And I'd have to try to explain to them that it was a separate night we were trying out using the venue. It was only a while back in the early 2000s, but it's amazing how much things have already changed. Now, I probably wouldn't have had to explained it as you get a real mixed bag of people going to gay bars these days.

The owner of that place was hard work. Whilst he was letting me use the venue, he wanted me to pay for half the advertising costs and split fees with me. It wasn't enough that people were coming into the venue, paying for entry and putting drinks money behind the bar, on a day where usually he wouldn't be open. On the odd occasion when work was dead and girls were complaining, I had issues trying to get the house fee off the girls (I think I charged £25). I thought to myself "no one complains about paying the fees in London, they usually lose their job otherwise". But things were different here. I was a small fish in a big pond, standing up for myself, with some girls older than me and with more dancing experience who thought they could just bully me into them not paying.

I honestly didn't realise how stressful it would be, and this was just my *first* regular bar event. I have no idea how I coped. Monday would come and my stomach would tighten up in knots, worrying whether girls would cancel last minute, whether we'd get enough customers, questioning whereabouts I should flyer this week. I danced there myself if anyone dropped out but a venue farther up the road where I worked wasn't happy and said I had to choose between them or the new club. I chose them, and continued to run the club night on the quiet, with the support of the owner knowing the situation. That in itself would make me nervous. But I didn't want to lose money from either. The original venue was my bread and butter money, the new club was the beginning of the empire I wanted to build.

A couple of local newspapers and a radio station jumped on board with a story of a local girl opening a pole dancing academy. I was bringing it to Kent and ladies were curious about how it could make them more confident, and possibly earn them money. I had girls contact me from ages 18-45; university students, wanting to earn a good wage in a short space of time whilst they studied, bored housewives wanting to do something to make them feel sexy, girls who had been cheated on by their boyfriends with an "I'll show you what you missed out on" attitude, and mothers wanting to get back into work around babysitters.

Those who wanted to train to do it as a career wouldn't be exclusive to Shimmer, so when I taught and gave handouts I listed venues or agencies they could try, if they wanted to branch out further than Kent. As time went on and I ended up signing more and more dancers to my agency, I began to look again in *The Stage* newspaper and online on strip forums, to see which other venues were advertising for dancers and would contact them to see if they would consider using an agency for help. Some said yes, and we would come to agreements regarding pay.

There was one issue that actually started costing me money though. I lost work dancing at other venues as I needed to be on standby in case anyone dropped out of one of my jobs last minute. And it did happen. A lot. I didn't want to have a contract taken away from me, but at the same time I also didn't really care for dancing at my own venues too much as I needed to have the respect of owning the agency, not being naked around all the people who knew I ran it. The pubs only had between two and four girls dancing per shift, so I needed to have a good rotation of girls, rather than me popping up every week.

In this industry, girls are flaky as fuck. Pardon my French. If they'd had a heavy night of partying, if they'd earned a lot of money the night before and "don't feel like coming in," they would cancel. That's sometimes why there's a large turnaround of staff, they'd piss everyone off and then have to move onto pastures new. I would charge them full house fee if they cancelled last minute and I'd keep a note of how many times they'd do it. Once a while due to illness, it can't be helped, but you can usually tell when a girl's lying. Lying is disrespectful, so I'd fire them immediately. They might be self-employed and have freedom as to when to work, but when they'd accepted a shift they should have the decency to work it.

Due to having to cover my own shifts, I really needed to be available to the Monday club (I had about six girls working per night there, so I blended in more than the two girl only venues). I handed in my notice after Christmas at the other club and explained why. We parted on good terms and they wished me well. It was a gamble leaving, but my agency wouldn't stand a chance if I couldn't supply enough girls.

The pressure of no longer creeping around and working for both companies was a relief. I was able to advertise the Monday club easier than before. I had also told a few of my customers discretely why I was leaving the other club, in case they'd wondered where I had gone to and to let them know that there was another venue in the area. I didn't overstep the mark by handing them leaflets, I just told them verbally, although I wasn't sure whether they'd remember or not as they'd had a few drinks by then!

So imagine my surprise when three of them turned up one night; Josh, Tim and Mark.

They were some of the younger guys I used to dance for – in their early 20s. Josh was absolutely stunning. He was just over six feet tall, with blonde hair and the most beautiful blue eyes and was always really well dressed. A few of the girls who had met them before from the other venue went over to talk to them. I was sitting at the end of the bar and waved. Josh came over:

> "Hey!" I said, as I leant forward to kiss him on the cheek "'It's so nice that you came down and remembered we were open!"

> "Well," he said confidently, "how else was I going to ask you out on a date? You didn't give me your number before you left the other venue" …

9

JOSH

The dancers' golden rule is:

"Act available but never be available"

It was drummed into us from the start. We are never supposed to date anyone we meet from work. We are also not supposed to exchange contact details with customers for two reasons. The first is a safety issue; leave the customers at the club, so they don't know anything about our private lives and therefore don't have the opportunity to become crazy stalkers. The second is because (according to licensing laws) it is classed as prostitution.

Josh

Venues have always indicated in their contracts that swapping numbers could be seen as trying to meet a customer outside of work and "continuing" the dances you had in the club. Guys proposition girls a lot of the time at work and some expect more after hours, whereby they can meet somewhere where there are no rules to break, where they can touch, or the girl can even offer extras. Not every girl sticks to the rules and if they have the opportunity to make more money outside of the club, then some go for it. However, if the club finds out, the dancer could lose their job and the club could lose its licence.

I mean, a girl could just want to keep in touch with a customer to tell him when she is next in the club, or even to go on a proper date if she genuinely likes the guy. But it's a hard thing to prove that that would be the only intention. Some of the London clubs even had "secret shoppers," who would set up gents going into the club, posing as clientele, to see if any girls would bend the rules. I heard at one point that two rival lap dancing clubs would send people into the other's venues!

It's harsh. *But,* and it's a fairly big but; it can't be avoided and girls will always break the rules. In the larger clubs, it may only be a matter of time until someone in charge finds out. In the smaller venues, not so much and *if* they know it's to inform a customer of when a girl is working, then they tend to turn a blind eye.

It's a difficult one, but girls *do* date people from work. When you work a great deal of unsociable hours per week, including weekends and so don't get to go out, the options for meeting somebody outside of work can be minimal. I know a few dancers over the years who have dated customers, some who ended up getting married. Having said that though, I also know guys who *only* date strippers, and that's not so cool.

The first "customer" I dated, was Josh.

I guess when he asked me on a date, despite the fact I'd met him as a customer in a different venue, I didn't feel like it was wrong to say yes; I was now the boss after all so I could bend the rules. Plus I was impressed he'd made the effort to come and find me at another venue to ask me out.

If Hugh Grant and Will Young could breed and have babies, Josh would have been the result. He looked a perfect combination of the two. He was also well spoken and his eyes sparkled when he smiled. So naturally, I gave him my number and he rang me the next day, suggesting we arrange to go to dinner.

Nothing was too much trouble for Josh. I told him I was vegetarian and he rang around numerous restaurants to check out their menus. He went out of his way to organise the perfect date. That impressed me. About six months prior I'd spent some time with another guy for a bit and he smoked so much weed that he rarely made the effort to do anything; including ringing me to check I was ok after he'd heard I'd been in a car accident. Now I had a guy, an extremely good looking one at that, and a gentleman by first impression, who wanted to give 100% even on a first date. I don't think it's ever happened to me since either.

He picked me up and took me to a really lovely Chinese restaurant, where we chatted for hours. He was a beer merchant and worked all over Kent, selling to pubs and bars. He was an only child, self-sufficient, living on his own and didn't take drugs.

We had our first kiss in the car when he dropped me off home and the whole date was just lovely. The next morning he rang me to see when we could meet up again. I was pretty busy that week but I had a couple of hours free one afternoon so he came and picked me up for lunch. The minute I got in the car he kissed me. I liked that. For the first time in ages I felt wanted.

We continued to date, and without fail, he'd always ring me in the morning to wish me a good morning. He was polite and so unbelievably sweet to me. We were such a whirlwind romance. People said that whenever I talked about him my eyes would light up. We fell for each other hard and quick. Valentine's Day arrived and Josh wanted to take me out to dinner again. We'd only been dating for three weeks. While I was getting ready, there was a knock at my door.

My doormat was covered with gifts – a card, a bunch of flowers (including three red roses, to represent the three weeks we'd been together), champagne, chocolates and perfume. Josh was hiding round the corner and watched me grin from ear to ear when I saw what he had left me. The whole night was perfect.

It didn't bother him that I danced. He'd come down most Monday nights to the club and bring friends along for the other girls to make money. If I wasn't dancing we'd sit at the end of the bar, flirting outrageously. When I stressed over my agency and spent too much time on the phone or the computer with emails and research, I could tell it bothered him a little as he'd come to spend time with me, not with my work – but he never said a word and just let me get on with it. And as he was a beer merchant, he began to ask proprietors of certain bars if they'd be interested in having dancers in their establishments to help raise their income. He helped me immensely to boost my business and I got some really good contracts because of him. Josh and I made a great team.

I even brought him along to the models parties in London, with a friend, and he understood when I'd need to walk off, mingle and act available (even though I wasn't) for the clientele and photographers. He understood completely where I was coming from. He was never jealous or stroppy at events.

I did begin to discover, though, that he was bragging about dating a lap dancer and model.

I'd just landed a job from an agency to do a TV advertisement for an adult channel. It was a full day's work, whereby I had to go in early to have my hair and make up done by a makeup artist. Then I had to read text off an autocue, whilst wearing various underwear sets and talking into the camera, and do some takes topless. It was a long day but I really enjoyed it. When Josh picked me up, however, he kept saying:

> "I told the owner of [one or other establishment he was working in] that you were topless modelling for the TV today, then I saw my boss and told him, then I saw..."

and he just went on and on. I didn't like it. He loved me and I know now that that was his way of saying he didn't care what I did and was proud of me. But then I saw it as him making me look like a trophy. I pulled him up on it and to my knowledge he didn't do it again.

Things were great between us. Really great. Until I fucked it up.

Josh wanted us to go on holiday; a friend of his had a timeshare that needed using in Tenerife so we decided to go. We were eight weeks into our relationship, but we hadn't spent a whole 24-hour day together. Going away for a week was the dumbest thing we could have done. I can't be around someone like that non-stop for that length of time. It does my head in. I'd never had to spend that long with brothers/sisters/family as I'd always been alone, so I didn't know *how* to share my time with others.

After three days away with Josh I'd had enough and just didn't want to go and do anything, except come home. Work was stressing me out and I also had to sort out the Monday club whilst I was over there, which cost me a lot in phone calls and meant I couldn't relax by the pool with Josh. Dancing had been a bit bad before going away so I had no money with me to pay for anything and although Josh said he'd take care of everything, I hated asking for money for anything I wanted to buy – gifts, food, drink. I wasn't used to someone helping me out like he was doing. And he wanted to do it, but there was just something in me that made me feel like I shouldn't have been asking. I shouted at him over silly little things – I can't even remember what now. He never raised his voice back and was just lost for words most of the time. He probably didn't understand why I was being like that. He was everything a girl could want and more, and there I was, shouting at him. Probably because I felt like I was a failure, with no money and no idea how to cope with someone so nice, being there for me and treating me like a princess.

By the time we came back I asked him if he could give me a couple of days before I saw him again, to have a break from being joined at the hip and to get back on top of admin I needed to do. I had to hit reset before I went crazy. However, in under 24 hours he was at my door again, saying he missed me. Now to some people that would be sweet, but I just *really* needed a break. So I asked him again to back off a little and to just give me a few days' space. But it's the "push me pull you" effect – he was worried about losing me and just wanted to be there and I was worried about losing him if I was around him constantly because I felt stifled. He sent flowers saying "Miss you and thinking about you:" I saw that as him not listening to me yet again and threw them away with anger and frustration.

Now what I hadn't realised until I went to Tenerife with him, was that Josh was pretty insecure. During his school years he was overweight and was taunted for it. Now anyone can have a great upbringing at home, but as we all know, kids can be cruel and it was at school he suffered. I understood where he came from with that as I was also taunted for my size at school, as well as being the "different kid, living with her Granddad." I should have related to him. But I didn't.

114

For example, the untold amount of toiletries he took with him on holiday, (not just one hair styling spray, but several, for various different hair types – we were only going for a week), the way he was immaculately groomed at all times, now told me a different story. It was because of how body conscious he was. I had always thought I was the only one for all this time. The gifts he showered me with, the ultimately amazing things he did for me, were all for him seeking approval from me, or from my friends who would then say to him how nice he was. To be liked. He was a people pleaser, just like me. I loved him, but I just never compared my issues to his. If I had done, maybe things could have ended up being different.

We didn't break up out of frustration or misunderstanding. We broke up because I became the biggest bitch ever. And to this day, it's one of my biggest regrets.

I saw our whole relationship as a game. I spoke to him like crap, to see if he'd still come back, and he did. Every time. He'd pick me up and drive me to work sometimes, or we'd go out drinking or out for dinner and everything would be great until I would just change my mind over things I wanted to do, or would boss him about profusely. I can't even tell you one specific thing I did; it was a collection of things that all built up to become a great tower of acrimony. And I pushed and pushed. And pushed. And every time, he remained, doing nice things for me and loving me.

Josh

I can probably guess what you're thinking:

"But did you *really* love him, seeing as you treated him that way?"

I did. I know I did. And to this day I don't know what I was playing at. What I thought I'd achieve by treating him so badly. He was the man who showed me how to love and be loved back and all I did was push him away. Until he was so far away he realised enough was enough. We broke up amicably one Monday and the next night he slept with someone else. I was crushed. Begged for him back but he said he just couldn't go through it again. And who could blame him really? He stayed longer than he should have. He moved on and I ended up having panic attacks because I was so upset, thinking of him with another girl, moving on without me, me not being with him. Karma got me back a good 'un. Claire still says to me now, laughing:

"You fucked that one up, didn't you!"

She's right. But I can't undo it and my lesson was learned. I never treated anyone like that again.

And Josh... if you ever do get to read this...just know that I'm sorry.
x

10

CLICK , SNAP , SHOOT

Luckily I had plenty of work to distract me after Josh, or I would have been miserable. With the Monday club, the Cellar bar contract he found me (they operated two nights per week with four girls) and two more pubs all in the same town, I controlled that area with dancers. The clientele called me "The Boss" or "The Pimp Mummy."

I had trained and employed a girl called Lydia and through working together we became good friends. We would tell guys we were cousins so we'd get asked to do double dances together (men loved the "keep it in the family fantasy," and it was more acceptable to them than wanting two sisters to dance, for instance). It boosted our money most nights. We began to work for a company that did masturbating videos, but there were no graphic "close ups" so we could stage the film to look like we were fingering ourselves, but we weren't. If we bent our middle finger, the guys would think our finger was in, when in fact it wasn't and our pussy was covered up with our whole hand. It was all an illusion.

The same company asked if Lydia and I would travel to their offices in Cambridge to do webcam work. We'd not done that before, and it *did* involve the insertion of toys (Continental modelling), but again there were no close ups and everything was shot from the side. If we wanted to, and we angled our legs correctly, we could still mimic the toy going in and out. The camera was also pretty far from the bed, and back then I'm also guessing the picture wasn't great quality like it is with webcams now. There was a chat room where we could type messages back and forth to the guys watching (there was no sound). Some would ask us about ourselves, and some would give us instructions for what to do. Some nights Lydia and I would work together. Other nights we'd travel up to Cambridge separately as they didn't always film a two-girl show.

Sometimes new guys would come into the chat forum, without saying hello and immediately message demands like:

"Stick your fist in"

And with much verbal abuse from the regular guys in the forum who were there to stay for quite a while, those new guys didn't stay long. They were more than likely on a budget, so were hoping to get to the nitty gritty quicker, rather than the sultry teasing followed by a lovely orgasm finale an hour later.

It wasn't anything to get upset over. I couldn't see these guys so if they said something rude it didn't affect me, unlike rude customers in dancing venues that you couldn't avoid for the rest of the shift. These men were virtual, so it was easier to have a thick skin doing webcam. The other perk of the job was that it was regular money, we were paid a set wage. When I used to drive Lydia she'd get on the wine and get a bit horny and start licking my pussy and *actually* fingering me, although one day I told her to ease up as she was wearing stick-on fingernails that were really sharp. The one on her index finger was loose and I was worried she'd end up losing it; I'd already been to the hospital once that year for cutting my tampon string too short at work (so it wouldn't show when I was dancing) and not being able to get that out. I didn't want to be known as the girl who's always in A&E with foreign objects stuck in her vagina.

Working with Lydia rather than working solo was more fun in that the time would go quicker; working alone meant I had to drag out the conversation and the show a bit more. But when it was just me, I had a friend who would drive me there, called Liam. He was a friend of the DJ from the Monday club and had a bit of a soft spot for me. Liam was great with me when I had panic attacks after my breakup with Josh. I remember once he tried to call me as he was in the area and wanted to pop round. I answered the phone and he could hear me hyperventilating. He sped round to my flat and just held me until my attack was over. He was really kind to me. We'd go clubbing with mutual friends on the weekends and when he dropped me off home, we used to have the odd kiss from time to time.

Liam and I enjoyed our road trips to my webcam job and always had a laugh. He drove me in his works van (he used to replace car windscreens) and a few times on the way home he'd pull off the road, down dirt tracks or into layby's unexpectedly and we'd fuck, with me riding him in the driver's seat and holding onto the caged bulkhead behind him for leverage. It was fun and exciting and I needed that after feeling so upset over Josh. The last thing I wanted was another full-on relationship.

****

Jobs came in thick and fast. Another colleague told me that camera clubs were always looking for models. Camera clubs consisted of photographers who took photos as a hobby. We called them "amateur photographers;" "togs" for short. Anything they shot was not to be used for publication, it was just for their projects. I

120

registered with two camera clubs in London. One (in South London) shot up to art nude, the other (East London) up to UK open leg. Togs had the opportunity to book us per hour to shoot one-to-one, or to come in on group shoot days, where there may be 10 to 15 other togs. It was usually down to the model to decide what to wear, and I always took a selection of clothes, uniforms, shoes and lingerie and sometimes I'd ask the photographers to choose as it always made them like you that little bit more. If they liked you, they'd book you again for a one-to-one. The club in South London was classier – the premises were cleaner, the togs were more into the arty stuff, just like if you were to pose nude for a still life art class, I guess. Working for amateurs was good practice for newer models like myself as it was always trial and error with posing and positions. They were not only interested in the model, but also the light, colours, textures and shapes. I remember I had a tog who was obsessed with triangles. Isosceles, Equilateral, Scalene and Obtuse. You name it, he loved them. Standing rigid with legs apart in an army outfit (the legs and floor forming a triangle) …sitting on my butt with my legs up and leaning back on my hands forming a V shape, although, it wasn't just a V…no no, it was a *"triangle."* I remember once I moved my arm back to adjust the waistband of an outfit and he blurted out excitedly:

"Stop there! Don't move! Your arm's bent – *there's a triangle!"*

A harmless guy, but a little ridiculous. Maybe he'd always wanted to be a geometry teacher, who knows.

It could have been worse. My friend Ariana was a well-known glamour model and she would work for professional and amateur togs. One day she had a job working up to American open leg level. So she's starting off in one outfit, slowly stripping down to nude, changing positions on the bed, sitting up, laying down, opening her legs wide. Whilst she was doing her thing and the tog snapped away, zooming in and zooming out with his big lens (no pun intended), she asked him if he'd be able to send her some photos for her portfolio. Sometimes amateurs would be happy to let us have a couple of their best pictures from the shoot, especially if we were polite to them. He said that would be ok and she gave him an address to send the photos too. This was before most cameras were digital and the majority of guys were still shooting with film. A few weeks later, she received a large thick envelope with the photographer's name on the back of it as the sender. Excited that he'd made such an effort to print up so many for her, and with the expectation that he must have shot with some really good results, she eagerly tore open the package. Much to her dismay, she was unable to use any of the 27 photos he'd taken of just her asshole.

Group shoots or one-to-ones, I didn't have a preference really. Whilst one-to-ones had fewer interruptions, group ones were more of a giggle because there were more guys. Beginning at one end of the room I'd look at one photographer and turn my head, body or both very slowly towards the other end of the room, so everyone would potentially get the chance of me looking into their camera. A bit like before with Jenna and Madison on the streets of London with the paparazzi. Then I'd move and do the similar thing back to the other side of the room, and so on and so forth. Standing, sitting up, twisting half my body towards the camera, laying back, bending over, arching my back, legs crossed, legs apart, smirking, smiling with my eyes wide, pouting whilst narrowing my eyes, biting my lip, opening my mouth with my eyes closed for the "ecstasy" look whilst I'd run my hands through my hair or slowly stroke various parts of my body. It was almost mechanical. On occasion I'd ask for requests.

Between my outfit changes, the photographers would change the colour of the backdrop or simply the props – perhaps to a wicker peacock chair (nearly every studio had one), or something to match the next costume change; for example if I was wearing a school uniform, they'd put a desk in shot. Props were always fun, and even hand-held props like books to cover up body parts when naked for cheeky type shots worked. But the time always went faster in group shoots, which were about three – four hours long. Sometimes they'd arrange an outdoor shoot on the grounds of a large country house. They'd book four or five models and the organiser would take each girl to a different part of the grounds once she was in her desired outfit. The togs would wander from one place to another at their leisure. One of us might be lying by the pool, another on a blanket in a field, one on a motorbike and one by an outdoor dining area. Whatever we were wearing didn't necessarily match the scenery, which I always thought odd, but hey, they didn't seem to care and we were paid quite a tidy sum for a six hour day.

Most of the amateur togs were of retirement age. Some had camcorders and would just wander around holding them, which I never understood really as they were just watching a girl do a sequence of poses. Most shot on film, but there were guys who didn't even have films in their cameras and just pretended to take photos all day. My guess is that they were either there for the role play fantasy, the "photographer and the model," or maybe they just couldn't print up any films because their wives would go ape shit.

You could hear the ones without film. The button didn't sound any different, but when you have film in a camera, you can hear the film wind onto the next frame. Without the film, the sound is different. It doesn't stop at the next frame because there isn't one. I just used to smile at them and wonder if they realised I knew they were just using the camera as their golden ticket to enter the shoot and look at nude women - but it was never discussed.

Working with all these photographers, I found another resource for my agency. I could now offer to the girls already on my books the chance of modelling for amateur togs, as well as any other dancers I met along the way. I would only tell the nice photographers and not the overly perverted ones, as I didn't want girls getting creeped out. I always wanted them to feel comfortable so they'd say I was a good boss who looked after her staff. So I printed up a list of girls on my books, with their stats and what they would be happy to model up to. I had different girls working up to different levels. The photographers would pay me a percentage per model, so I was once again in a win-win situation.

I felt like us dancers and models lived in such a different world. And it was, but it was *our* different world. I never stopped trying to develop my agency. I never knew if work would go quiet, so it was best to keep it going. One day I had a call from the paper affiliated with the Essex club, the first people I ever modelled for:

'Hi Holly. We're working on a new project. How would you like to be a TV presenter?"

11
GIRL CHANNELS

The newspaper was a flagship for many things; the Essex club I had danced in, a nude magazine, an adult film company, a string of sex shops and now a new TV channel. The channel was to run seven nights per week, from 8 until 3am. Its formula was to have two girls presenting the show live, whilst viewers could text in to communicate with them and the girls would read out the messages. After 10pm, the girls could go topless – if, for instance, they received a certain amount of text requests to do so. In addition, there was an option for guys to call in and chat to one of three other girls working that day who were also visible on the TV. So basically the company made money on the text messages, which cost about £1.50 per text and a couple of pounds per minute with the chat lines. Both

Girl Channels

Lydia and I were asked to work for the Girl Channel. They paid a nightly rate, paid our cabs home and offered us at least two nights per week. We would finally have a really stable income and it was too good an opportunity to turn down.

The format regarding the request side of things, was kind of similar to the webcamming I did in Cambridge, except on the TV we weren't nude, and we had a moderator scrutinising the texts before allowing them to come up on the TV screen. For viewers at home, the layout of the show would be the two presenters in the top left hand corner of the TV screen, with text messages moving underneath, and down the right hand side of the screen there were three boxes, with a girl in each box on a phone, waiting for viewers to call up and talk to them. The longer the guys stayed on the phone, the more money the company made. They would rotate the five of us each day from presenting, to going onto the phones. Our phone calls were also moderated and we weren't allowed to talk about anything too rude. and when we talked live we weren't allowed to swear. The company didn't want to face a fine.

There was a shift change after the first hour as some girls didn't want to do the topless shows – these girls mainly lived in London as an hour's work was worthwhile for them with fewer travel costs. After 1am, three girls would leave and the two remaining would do the final show, with one on the phone and one presenting and reading the text messages.

It was *really* fun. Sometimes we'd pre-plan and decide to all wear similar themed outfits like doctors and nurses for instance. Friends would text in to tell us they were watching, so they could get a mention. Sometimes we'd say:

> "We need 50 more texts saying 'Boobs out' before we get our boobs out tonight boys"

or words to that effect, to boost the money generated through text messages.

It always seemed to be me that ended up having practical jokes played on her on live TV. Some days, for instance, one of us presenting on the sofa had to have our hands tied behind our back whilst we were bent over and lightly spanked; the one who had the most votes was the chosen one. It always ended up being me. I swear the moderators rigged it. There was another day where I worked alongside Brandy, a girl with huge boobs; I think she was at least a 30JJ, with a tiny waist which made her look even more top heavy. We discussed on the programme how heavy her boobs were and I made a joke about how it wouldn't surprise me if they could give someone a concussion if you hit them hard enough in the head. So we were egged on by the cameramen to try it out, with Brandy smacking me in the head with one of them. And yes, I can confirm it was a pretty heavy boob. But it didn't stop there, the cameramen and moderator were laughing so much at how it looked, they wanted her to repeat it so I said:

"Guys, if you want to see me get hit in the head again by Brandy's boobs, text in 'Boob smack' (shaking my head at the same time, telling them not to encourage it)."

Regardless of whether or not anyone texted in, the moderator was typing so it filled up the screen and I didn't stand a chance of not getting hit in the head again. I got boob-smacked in the head about four times that night. Luckily I didn't have concussion by the end of the evening (imagine having to explain that at the doctor's the next day).

Friends assumed being on the girl channels would automatically make me famous. But although the channel was available to most people for free, not everyone watched it. I guess you could say I was now semi-famous in the glamour industry. But if I walked down the street in the daytime no one would recognise me, although that's probably because I've always been happy to go out with glasses and no make-up when it's my day off – I've always managed to blend into a crowd. I did feature in the paper more, if I was scheduled to

be on TV there'd be a photo of me in the paper that same day –
sometimes a whole page. I remember someone telling me that Josh
couldn't seem to get away from me, what with being in the paper,
on live TV in the evening, the TV ad I did when I was with him and
I'd also taken part in a fly-on-the-wall documentary about strippers
before I was with him and that was just being aired. It was like his
ex-girlfriend was stalking him through all forms of media and he
couldn't escape.

Lydia, on the other hand, *did* get recognised, even in the
supermarket. Guys were always coming up to talk to her, but I think
she revelled in it. Being on the TV changed her. Her attitude, the
way she spoke to people became really brash. Like she thought the
TV really made her something. She was a topless TV presenter for
goodness sake, but she was acting like she was an A-list celebrity.
Now, when she danced in my venues, she started to talk to the other
girls like they were beneath her because she was on the TV. The
girls complained to me. We were also allowed to consume alcohol
on the girl channel, as long as it wasn't evident, but Lydia started to
drink *a lot* and by the time she and I were doing the very late show,
I had to carry the whole show because she was so intoxicated. She'd
be just about conscious sitting on the sofa, swaying, slurring and
doing everything super slow and not conversing with me. How she
didn't get fired I have no idea. She rang me the next day to laugh
about it and I pointed out to her that if she ever did that to me again,

we would fall out. I struggled to deal with drunks. It was hard enough to deal with them as customers. Happy drunk is fine, but moody drunk is not good, especially when it affects your work.

When we took phone calls on the programme we'd get a lot of guys giving us instructions to confirm it was actually us they were speaking to. Conversations would usually begin with:

"I don't believe it's you – give me a wave to prove it."

But there was a five second delay, and we had to keep reiterating this to them. Some would ring to just give orders like "wave, bounce up and down on the bed" or "bend over and shake your ass" and they would start to laugh excitedly as we complied, as if they were looking at women for the first time or playing their first game of Simon Says. Some would ask for us to get our boobs out and we'd flash them briefly, as we wanted more people to ring and request us to do it several times over (the money was important for the company), rather than have them out on display for too long. For the leg men, we'd ask the cameraman to pan the camera up and down from our feet to the top of our butts (each girl in the box on the screen had her own cameraman). But we also had a few lonely guys ringing, just to talk. It was a lot of money for a chat, but these guys didn't even ask us to get our boobs out. We just looked at the camera from time to time, smiling, waving and moving around a little (so more people would get in the queue to call and not think we were just motionless and boring) and these guys would just talk to us about their lives and how their day was.

A really old guy used to call up, called Walter, whose wife had died and he'd not really been out much since she died, so talking to us on the TV made his day and gave him something to look forward to. I thought this was really sweet. As the weeks progressed Walter sent us all gifts of jewellery – nice jewellery, not cheap or tacky, to say how much he appreciated us being there to talk to him. The calls were more personal to guys like Walter, as they were having a one -to-one conversation with us. The Channel had a PO Box where fan mail could be sent and each model had a pigeonhole where we could collect it. I took the time to read every letter I received which were all polite and guys were so complimentary. Some of them sent photos of themselves with their letters and a description and I wondered if this is how dating agencies first started out with putting couples together.

I wrote back to my "fans" (that sounds so weird even now), and enclosed a signed photo of myself.

One thing I learned working on the Channel was how many men were actually obsessed with feet and shoes. Whether we were presenting or on the phones, we'd receive untold amounts of text and telephone demands/requests (depending on how polite they were), all involving feet. There was an endless list, some of which included:

Dangle our shoes off our big toe
Shoes off to go barefoot
Shoes off to see our stockinged feet
Shoes on to see heels
Rub our legs and feet/shoes
Look at the dirty soles of our shoes
Look at our wrinkled soles of our feet
Look at our painted toenails
Tell them on camera to lick our shoes or feet
There was always something, and most of the time on text they'd add "Mistress" to our names…

"Mistress Holly can you please do (xyz)."

It was their way of saying, "we're asking nicely so please do this for us." Those who used to ring in would say how they'd love to come and kiss or lick our feet and some would proposition us, asking if we could actually meet up with them so they could "foot worship" a glamour model.

And this was how I discovered "Foot Worship" was actually a thing…

12

FOOT FETISH

F oot fetish, foot worship or podophilia; they all boil down to the same thing: feet. Obviously not all men love feet (and it is more of a male thing than a female thing) but apparently it's the most common sexual fetish for a non-sexual body part.

I mean, I'd known guys to have a foot fetish when I danced, but more the odd one here and there. Now I was exposed to it every night that I was on TV and it became a revelation to me that it was pretty normal. And when I met up with my old friend Michelle for lunch – who I'd known since I was a teenager, she asked me whether the whole foot thing grossed me out. I told her I didn't think so.

Foot Fetish

"You know I go to fetish parties, right?' she asked

"No, I'd no idea."

"Well, I've actually been on the fetish scene for years and I'm a part time Dominatrix'"

She had a normal day to day job but this was her day-off go-to.

"I'm actually going to a foot fetish party in a couple of weeks. Do you want to come along? It's full of foot slaves, foot Mistresses and it's quite a good night."

(A foot slave worships the feet and the foot Mistress is (obviously) the female doing the dominating.)

I mulled over it for a few days but said I didn't want them licking my feet or sucking my toes, but foot massages and the like would be ok.

"You can do what you want – you're in charge of the situation; *you're* the Mistress." Michelle smiled.

I thought what the hell, it'd get me out of the house and may be educational, seeing as I talked to so many foot fetish guys on the phones. And I trusted Michelle. I mentioned a couple of times on the TV that I was going to a foot fetish party and guys would phone into the show to ask me details. Whether or not they'd turn up I didn't know, as they had to pay for entry.

I met Michelle at the train station and we went to her house to get ready.

"I've got us a driver today, he's one of my slaves, and turning up in half an hour or so. Have you painted your toenails?" I nodded at her. "Ah that's a shame, I'm allowing him to paint mine for me when he gets here."

We applied our make up – very dark eyeshadow and deep red lipstick. We both decided to wear black, me a long, see-through asymmetrical dress with long sleeves and with leather bikini underneath, finished off with platform thigh boots, and Michelle a short strappy dress with black strappy heels to match.

The buzzer to her apartment sounded.

"Yes?" she answered sternly

"It's me, Mistress."

"Did you bring wine?"

"I did, Mistress."

"Then you can come up"

A middle-aged man came to the door with wine and Michelle introduced him.

"This is Slave. Slave, this is Mistress Holly."

"Hello Mistress"
I said hello back

"Now please open the wine and pour us both a glass. You can have a soft drink from my fridge because you're driving."

"Yes, Mistress."

I let Michelle do most of the talking to the slave so I could absorb what she was doing and be able to follow suit once we got to the party. I sipped the wine he gave me and watched him concentrate on painting her toenails.

"Now make sure you don't make a mess of it" she demanded "I want them looking perfect."

"Yes Mistress."

He concentrated hard. I could tell he didn't want to disappoint Michelle. He was, after all, here to serve her.

Other than giving him instructions, Michelle and I spoke to each other, almost as though he wasn't there. He was one of her "regular slaves" who used to drive her to events. She had a coffle of slaves at her beck and call and would pick and choose at her leisure which one she wanted to use. She even allowed some of them to clean her house. After all, they didn't cost her anything; oftentimes they would bring *her* a gift for the pleasure.

Once her toenails had dried, she allowed him to put her shoes on her and do up the buckle. He then picked up our bags to carry them to the car and held every door open for us. I had a coat to cover up my suggestive outfit from the public eye, until we reached our destination. It was still light and I didn't want to get stared at in the streets.

Foot Fetish

The club for the event was below some railway arches. It really fitted the atmosphere – underground and hidden. Once we entered the slave walked off with a bag and left us.

"Where's he going?" I asked Michelle

"He's gone to get changed. A lot of people don't like walking around outside in their gear – they have lockers and such in here so people can store their day clothes away. Let's go sit down."

We sat on a sofa and Michelle could see I was a little nervous. Men and Mistresses started to arrive, not all together, and some greeted each other whilst some men (or slaves, even if they didn't yet know they were slaves) sat on the side lines. You could tell which guys had been before as they wore some sort of fetish attire, the others just wore jeans and t-shirt, but I could see there were more regulars than newbies. Fetish attire is much easier for women: anything black, pvc, leather, rubber or kinky looking. For the men it's mainly black again, leather or rubber trousers, fishnet or mesh vests, long black leather coats – it depends. If he's a male Dom (and you do get them), they tend to wear more. If he's a slave or very submissive he'll wear a little less – maybe short rubber shorts, topless with a dog collar or some sort of restraints. Michelle's slave showed his face and was wearing leather trousers and a harness on the top half of his torso. He fell to his knees in front of me:

"Mistress, can I get you a drink?"

"I'd like a glass of rosé wine please."

"Make that two" Michelle added

"Yes Mistress" and he got up and walked off to the bar.

Two men sat in silence together on the opposite sofa, staring at us.

"You two!" Michelle pointed at them. They sat up straight through fear. "Get over here and kiss my feet!"

They jumped up out of their seats, eyes wide with excitement and bounded over, got down on their knees and bent down to kiss a foot each whilst she still wore her shoes. They delicately kissed from toe to heel to ankle. She turned to me:

"That's all there is to it."

"Well I don't want to take my boots off."

Foot Fetish

"That's fine." she said.

Our wine arrived and we thanked Michelle's slave. She allowed him to mingle around, unlike some Mistresses. He knew I was new to all this so asked:

"Mistress Holly, may I clean your boots with my tongue?"

I looked down at him on his knees and replied

"You may, but only below the knee."

I didn't want any of the men there getting too eager if they headed towards the top of my thigh area.

'Thank you, Mistress.'

With my legs crossed I raised one, and he held the heel of my boot whilst he licked the back of it. I told him the front was dirty and needed to be shined up and he moved his mouth around to the toe of the leather. Once I'd felt like he'd done enough, I suggested he move onto the next boot, to clean it just as well as the first, and with utter contentment he proceeded to do so.

"I'm bored," said Michelle.

144

She'd already told the two guys to leave and had been chatting to me whilst Slave had been tongue polishing my boots.

"Shall we take a wander?" I nodded and dismissed the Slave.

We walked into a different tunnel where men were lying on their backs next to each other, on a large, embroidered rug. Mistresses were standing around, chatting. Chains were set into the opposite ends of the walls and hung down slightly.

"This is the trampling room" Michelle stated. "You can either leave your boots on or take them off."

She began to undo her buckles.

"Barefoot is definitely easier for this though. Watch…"

She pulled herself up onto the chains and stood on a guy. *Now* I began to understand what the chains were for – stability. Using the men as uneven stepping stones, she walked from one to the other, whilst they laid completely still. Once she walked across all of them, she turned, walked halfway back and stopped on a guy in the middle, taking the time to walk up and down on him. All over his chest, sometimes stomach, sometimes on his ball area.

Foot Fetish

The stomach is a difficult area to walk on as it's softer and therefore not as sturdy. If you're careful, you won't cause damage. Obviously bare feet can cause less damage because the surface area is larger than, say, the heel of a shoe. The smaller the surface area, the harder the pressure. I remember that from physics class at least, although they always used the question:

> "What would cause more damage to a varnished floor, an elephant or a lady in stilettos?'

Maybe they should have changed it to:
> "What is more likely to pierce a lung…a lady trampling on someone's rib cage in stilettos, or a lady trampling with bare feet?"

If you jump on a guy hard, then obviously you've a chance of cracking a rib. If you're wearing very sharp heels and do that, then you could possibly pierce the heart, lung or liver, depending on where you're standing of course. It's about common sense. And standing on a windpipe would just be plain idiotic. You don't want a corpse on your hands. With regard to the stomach, the guy should tense the muscles to protect the spleen, but as I said, barefoot on the stomach is difficult enough, let alone with shoes on.

Michelle was enjoying herself, so I unzipped my boots and joined her, hoisting myself up. House music blared from the speakers and I marched up and down on the spot on one guy to the beat, then moved onto another. The human carpet lay there patiently waiting for the promise of a pair of feet to spend time on them. More Mistresses joined, sometimes two on one man, some slapping guys in the face with the soles of their bare feet and some trampling with their shoes on.

After a few minutes I jumped off and went to put my boots back on for a while for a breather when a guy standing by the wall wearing a toga walked over to me.

"I really like your boots, Mistress. If I lie down will you stand on me wearing them? Just on my chest, and make me lick your heels? I really want to suck on them."

"Sure" I said, making out like this was perfectly normal. "Lie down".

He joined the end of the human carpet. Thank goodness those chains were there or I would have fallen off. My boots were about 6 inches high, with a 2-inch platform at the front. They weren't stilettos, they were around an inch square, so no chance of puncturing anything. Standing on his chest, pacing on him, putting most of the weight on

147

the toe of my shoe, he stared up at me, with a light smile on his face. Transferring all the weight to one foot, I raised my other leg and hovered my boot over his mouth, still hanging on with the chains. I placed the side of my boot to his mouth, and he kissed and licked it, then placed the ball of the boot on his cheek and lightly put the tip of my heel up to his lips. He opened them, ready to receive my heel and I stuck about an inch in. He licked the tip and side and then sucked on it as I moved my heel slowly in and out of him. He was giving head to my boot.

I know what you're probably thinking: "This guy is sucking and licking *a boot*. What about germs?!"

Foot lovers, at least the majority I've met, love dirty shoes, dirty soles of bare feet, sweaty socks and sweaty feet. They just don't care. I've no idea why. Maybe it's the whole being made to feel inferior or feel degraded. They all have preferences though. For instance, some like painted toenails whilst others only like girls with plain toenails to avoid the possibility of varnish chipping in their mouth if they're sucking on toes.

I walked past the "food room" – where the floor was covered with plastic sheeting and bowls of frozen fruit and cream. Mistresses dipped their toes in and men were licking it off, enjoying the sweet feast. I decided that definitely wasn't for me. Too much. So Michelle and I went to sit either side of a Mistress, Stephanie, who Michelle already knew. There was a man lying at her feet on the floor and she gently had her feet placed on him with her very pointy toed heels. Whilst they chatted, Michelle called a slave over to become her human footstool. He got on all fours and Michelle elevated her feet. The slave beneath Stephanie shouted up to her whilst she was talking:

"Did I say you could interrupt!?" She looked down at him.

"No, Mistress."

"Well then, be quiet."

She stomped her feet on his chest lightly as a punishment. He obeyed, and didn't speak again, unless he was spoken to.

The Footstool's friend came over to me and asked if he could kiss my feet, not my boots. Feeling more relaxed now I'd been here for a couple of hours, I gave in and was ready to allow my bare feet to be touched. I let him unzip my boots.

"I've seen you on the TV Channel and was excited to hear that you were going to be here tonight, Mistress Holly."

Foot Fetish

Revealing my bare feet, he grinned and face planted the soles, remaining there for a few seconds with his eyes closed, and a smile of gratification. He began to butterfly kiss them, working his way from the heel, to the arch, ball of my foot to my ankles and bridge. He paid attention to every area, he didn't miss one inch of skin. He held onto one foot with both thumbs on the ball of it and kissed my big toe. He slowly took the whole toe in his mouth and sucked it, like the heel sucker before, then licked in between each toe, before placing all toes in his mouth at once and French kissing them all. It wasn't as bad as I thought; it was bearable, but it did feel strange. Wet, obviously, like stepping in warm sand at the beach where the tide had gone out. I much preferred the trampling.

"I knew you'd change your mind and let someone do it eventually." Michelle smiled, her feet still on the human footstool.

I giggled back at her.

Whilst I let the foot licker continue, I noticed in the corner of the room a guy and a girl lounging on beanbags. Michelle nodded over to him and said to me:

"He's a Master, he likes feet but goes for something different, watch…"

He grabbed one of the girl's feet and as he put her heel in his mouth, he began to use his teeth. She screamed, laughed, wriggled, but he wouldn't let go. He wasn't breaking the skin or hurting her. He was tickling her. He had a tickle fetish. Again something I'd never heard of before that night. I *hate* tickling, but some people apparently get pleasure out of the torture, the helplessness of it, of receiving it; whilst others, like the Master here got off on the control of it, making someone writhe and kick whilst he had a hold of her foot. Foot slaves stood against the wall and spectated, some getting aroused watching the girl roll around on the bean bag laughing uncontrollably. Turns out that same Master produced tickling films for sale and he was making a pretty tidy sum.

Michelle's slave came and sat next to me. First impressions can be pretty judgemental and maybe I expected someone with a different fetish to have had a weird upbringing, or be a little, well, "simple". But there were so many people here, from all walks of life. And what exactly *was* the norm? Right here, it was feet. But outside, in the real world, what floats everyone's boat can be really different and I was starting to realise this. "Vanilla lifestyle" is a reference to "standard sexual practice," with nothing "weird," but what classes as *weird* really? Is vanilla just having sex in the missionary position? Or having sex with more than one person at a time? Because if you think about it, one person may think that even missionary sex is weird and that having sex with more than one person at a time is normal for them. And it's the same with feet. Someone with a fetish for feet, well that's *their* "standard sexual practice," and therefore *their* vanilla. Michelle's slave had a high profile job in the city. I wanted to talk to him for a moment, casually, rather than with the Mistress/Slave tone:

"So," I dismissed the other slave with my hand who was still tonguing my toes, whilst I addressed Michelle's slave: "how long have you been into this kind of thing for? I'm curious."

"Well all my life I've just liked feet. I can't recall anything in particular that triggered my desire. I can only explain it to you, in the same way as to why people like chocolate. And that's to say, *I just do*."

I never thought of it like that until he said it. Sometimes we *do* just like things we do, without rhyme or reason. *But* some do have reasons which I discovered through talking to an old school friend with a vivid memory. He recalled us play-fighting on the floor and me backing him into a corner and putting my feet in his face whilst wearing white knee high socks. That's his first recollection of feet and he's had a fascination with feet since, especially feet in white socks.

Clearly the role of foot Mistress was set within me from a young age and I didn't even know.

13
HAPPY BIRTHDAY TO ME

With my workload expanding, I took my Auntie Dee on board to be in charge of the agency bookings. The girls would ring and confirm their shifts and Dee would rebook if there was a problem. This freed up my time and made things easier especially when I was working late nights. Dee concentrated on the dancers whilst I booked in the models for the amateur Togs. She lived just up the road from Granddad.

At the foot fetish party I met a Master who arranged smaller parties for foot lovers and paid girls to attend, plus me for booking them. Not all the dancers I knew wanted to do it, so I also booked cousins and friends who weren't in the industry, liked their feet being played with and were interested in earning extra money. The Master chose girls he liked by me emailing over photos of the girls' faces, feet and shoe sizes. The guys at these parties preferred the "girl next door" look. They were only interested in feet, so girls oftentimes just wore jeans and a nice top. Shoes weren't even a factor as most of the evening they ended up barefoot. I never attended as often I was already booked elsewhere, but supplying 10 girls at a time meant I was earning a tidy monthly sum.

The paper began to do a piece for pub and factory visits. Venues would request to book two models to pose topless with the pub landlord or some customers, and it would be printed in the paper for a bit of fun. This was in the day when a topless calendar on the wall of a men's workshop wasn't seen as offensive or misogynistic.

Knowing one of the paper's photographers quite well meant he would say to me:

> "Find me three venues, workshops or pubs and we'll shoot them all in one day."

It would just be a case of changing outfits in the car (usually just skirts or shorts as whatever we had on top always came off), so it looked like we'd done the visits on separate days. Three visits in a day meant we'd receive quite a good paycheque the following month. Lydia and I often did these shoots together as we were the most local to each other. We never ran out of venues because I always asked the pubs I put dancers in, who were always happy to have a bit of free advertising aimed at the male community. Workshops and factories were also easy as all I needed to do was announce in one of the strip pubs that the paper was looking to shoot two half-naked girls with some workmen and immediately customers would be on the phone to their bosses. In the pub visits, we'd generally be photographed pulling pints with a barman, then in a crowd with the patrons – and sometimes they were a bit drunk so we had to smile whilst thinking "who just pinched my butt?" and trying to slap away hands attempting a quick grope. In the factory or workshop visits, we'd pose on the work counters or stand beside the vendors, holding one of their products. I remember being in an ironmongery place and having to hold steel chains off a reel over my body, which were really cold. There's an art to smiling while hiding your discomfort.

Now I was on the TV and in the newspapers, it was *my* turn to have one of those model parties for my birthday. Jenna and I had a joint party as we were a few days apart, and she was much better known than I. It was to be held in a different club from the parties I'd been to before, but still in London's West End.

We had formal invitations printed and sent them out three weeks before. We booked a room each in a Mayfair hotel and a limousine to take us to the party, along with Lydia, another friend of mine Charlie, and Hannah, one of Jenna's best friends. I wore a fluorescent pink, see-through Lycra dress. It was pretty daring, but at these kinds of parties it didn't really matter, and after all I was one of the birthday girls and wanted to stand out. Jenna wore a very short white skirt and white bra top.

Nina the reporter showed up, as did photographers from the paper. Girls from the TV channels, dancers, ex boyfriends, friends from Kent and London, siblings, cousins and old school friends attended. My friends and family from the life outside of my glamour life found the evening highly entertaining, soaking up the atmosphere and watching models stop what they were doing to pose whenever photographers stood in front of them, then continue going about their evening the minute the pictures were taken. They made up a game which they called "spot the silicone." My ex-boyfriends were in their element with all the flesh on display.

Champagne flowed and Lydia and I tried toffee martinis at the bar. Television actors attended and at one point someone came up to me and said that a well-known singer was complaining upstairs that he wasn't being let in. Whilst the club had a separate restaurant and bar upstairs, to get into our event required having an invite to get a wristband, which he hadn't been allocated. He was pretty annoyed and despite his bad attitude I found one for him and his friend, without a thank you I hasten to add. There was no more room in the club – I couldn't believe it. There was a one in, one out policy – a line outside – to get into *our* party. It was *amazing*. I felt really important.

Nina wanted to create a story for the paper so my model friend Alicia suggested that we get it on in the girls' toilets whilst a photographer took some "exposed" pictures. A soap opera actor was tagging along with Nina to watch what was going on. Alicia and I didn't care; we were so drunk and loved kissing each other, that we just did what we did whilst the camera snapped away; getting our tits out and Alicia pretending to go down on me. It wasn't long until a member of club security came in and stopped the fun:

> "You need to get out," he remarked to the photographer and actor; "this toilet is for *ladies* only."

He was really pissed off with them, but completely unphased by me sitting on a toilet seat with Alicia's head between my legs.

They left hastily and we laughed, adjusted our clothes and followed them out. My male friends who weren't in the industry saw us all coming out of the toilets laughing and asked us what was going on.

"Oh, Alicia was just going down on me and the photographer was taking   pictures   and   we   got   in   trouble   with security…"

Their jaws dropped. Sometimes I forgot that to most people, this wasn't part of their everyday lives.

We danced, mingled, laughed and drank. Charlie went missing two thirds of the way into the night, which was standard procedure from her during a night out. She'd always ring a guy for a booty call once she'd had a drink. She used to say:

"I turn into a whore when I've had alcohol"

and I used to tell her:

"Darling, you can only call yourself a whore if you get paid for it, and you don't!" laughing.

Lydia started to become her usual absolute drunken mess and disappeared with the girl channel staff to an after party at the studio. I didn't want to go as I wanted to make the most of the fantastic hotel room I had booked for the night, plus I didn't want to have to deal with Lydia in that state and she could be someone else's problem.

As people began to leave, I stood on the stairs and looked around at everyone enjoying themselves. Taking in the atmosphere, one of my friends from Kent, Lucas, came and stood with me:

"Great party, Holly! Thanks for inviting me"

"You're welcome" I smiled.

"So where have Lydia and Charlie gone?"

"Lydia's gone on to another party and Charlie's gone to get laid. She always does!"

"Haven't you had any luck tonight then? On the man front I mean?"

"Nah. Haven't you pulled any girls?"

"Not tonight. To be honest I think I felt a bit intimidated by all these beautiful women in one room!"

I found that hard to comprehend. Women always admired Lucas. He had the most piercing blue eyes and dark hair. He and I had slept together once before, but we were such good friends that despite him looking great and being a great person to boot we just laughed at how incompatible we were in the bedroom. Something just didn't click with us.

We stood in silence, for a few minutes, sipping our drinks.

"It's a shame really, I was hoping to get laid for my birthday."

Then I looked at him and said quickly, before I changed my mind:

"Do you want to come back with me to my hotel room?"

"Really? After the disaster last time?"

"Well neither of us has any other option!"

We both laughed and snuck away a few minutes apart from each other so our mutual friends wouldn't see to start any gossip. His colleague had already got the train home so he didn't need to worry about him. We hopped into a cab as quickly as we could once we were outside, like two naughty teenagers trying not to get caught for misbehaving.

"I have to be back in Kent early as I have to start work at 8."

"No worries, I won't take offence, just set the alarm on your phone."

With Lucas' jacket over my shoulders, we staggered into the hotel lobby, where the bright lights fell harshly on our eyes and got the elevator to the floor of my room. Once we reached my hotel suite we began kissing, then Lucas ran off into the bathroom. I began to get undressed next to the king size bed but heard water running and headed towards the bathroom. He'd discovered the bathtub was also a jacuzzi and had got over excited with the amount of complimentary bubble bath.

"Let's have sex *in here*!" he exclaimed.

I was hesitant as I was allergic to most bubble baths and perfumed soaps. But it was my birthday, so I thought screw it (literally). We fucked in the jacuzzi, we fucked on the large sofa and finally, we fucked in the bed. I can't remember when we fell asleep, or even if we actually finished fucking to completion. I do remember, however, waking up at 8am, looking next to me and Lucas still being there. His alarm hadn't gone off.

"Lucas," I prodded him and he acknowledged me, with a short sharp "Mmm" sound, "didn't you need to be at work for 8am?"

"Mm"

"Well, it's 8am now."

"What!?" He sat bolt upright and fell onto the floor trying to get out of bed as his foot was caught in the bedsheets. "Fuck! My phone died!"

"Well, there's not much you can do now, you're already well and truly late" I said loudly, as he'd gone into the bathroom to pick his clothes up off the floor next to the jacuzzi.

"I'm going to have to get a cab there" he reappeared, doing up his belt. He leant over to me in bed and gave me a peck, "Thanks for a great night."

"You're welcome" I replied. I would have said "Anytime," but he and I both knew that wouldn't be true.

I fell asleep for another hour then showered and packed up my stuff. Lucas texted me to say he got into work, still in his clothes from the night before.

I had time to kill so I dozed on the sofa with the TV on until Jenna and Hannah knocked on my door. They were also feeling the effects of the night before as they'd stayed up late and had a bit of an after party in their room with a couple of other friends from the club.

"I didn't see you leave last night? Did you leave before us?" asked Jenna

"Yeah I called it a night around 2ish I think."

We headed down to reception, with me looking like a bag lady as I had Lydia and Charlie's belongings in tow as well as my own. They'd do their homing pigeon bit later to my flat no doubt once they surfaced from the evening – or early morning. As Jenna went to return their room key to check out, the receptionist said their room had been flagged up as having an issue and rang housekeeping to check.

"There's fake tan on the sheets, alcohol spilled everywhere, blood on one of the towels and a smashed glass" informed the receptionist.

One of the guys had cut his hand on the glass he broke and naturally used one of the small towels to stem the bleeding.

"Everything has to be incinerated as it's all ruined, and the carpet will have to be deep cleaned. We'll need £50 extra off you for damages."

The girls paid it and then we left to go home. Considering the hotel was an expensive one I'm surprised they didn't charge more than £50. It seemed that they were just looking for extra money. Any of those linens could have been washed on a hot wash (a standard hospitality industry requisite anyway) and the stains would disappear. Fake tan comes off easily – which is why it was on the sheets in the first place. Perhaps the blood may not have come off, but it was a face towel, easily thrown away, easily replaced. To be fair they probably would have tried washing it out anyway and kept the money.

"How come *you* never get in trouble!?" Hannah said to me in the cab to the station. "You just, go out, get drunk and go back to the hotel sensibly!"

I shrugged my shoulders and smirked, not telling them what I'd got up to. The only evidence left of my soirée was a few bubbles in the bottom of the jacuzzi tub, some tangled sheets and a sore vagina from an allergy to the bubble bath.

14
THE EMERALD ISLE

I decided with all the work I was getting that I wanted a newer car and a bigger flat as I wanted an extra room as an office. So I bought myself a black 4 x 4, had the windows tinted, bought a personal number plate *and* found a flat 5 minutes up the road from Granddad, which was handier as he had even more hospital visits to attend so it saved me a bit of travel time. The flat was double the size of my previous one, above my hairdresser's, walking distance to the town centre and train station, and close to every takeaway you could imagine. I was blessed with its location.

And then the Girl Channel fired me.

It stemmed from one night with the production staff refusing to close the windows, telling the girls there were no windows behind the backdrop, yet the backdrops were blowing about and we could hear the London traffic from the third storey up. Being cold on live TV made the girls in the little boxes visually uncomfortable on their beds, rather than sexy (except of course for more erect nipples). It wasn't *just me* complaining about the temperature in there, but I did make out I was using the covers on the bed as blankets, and covering myself up, whilst I was on the phones chatting to guys, covering only parts of me up at a time though (parts that probably actually didn't matter, a shoulder here and there, or my bottom half, sticking a leg out seductively from time to time). It didn't affect me or the company in that I wasn't getting phone calls, guys were calling up to talk to me and there were no waiting gaps on the line in between. After my shift I thought nothing more of my

"It's freezing, can you *please* close the windows" comments until the booker rang me the next day:

"Hi Holly, the manager thinks you should take some time out to sort yourself out after your issues last night."

"My *issues?* What, the issue that I was cold? I wasn't the only girl on set complaining about it. The production staff were trying to tell us there weren't any windows, let alone windows open, all because they couldn't be bothered to close them."

"Yes, you may not have been the only one complaining," she continued, "but we think you were the one instigating the problem."

I was shaking my head in bewilderment even though she couldn't see me.

"So what you're saying is…I was the one telling the girls to say they were cold, when in fact they weren't?"

She fell silent for a few seconds, realising that what she was saying didn't actually make sense, even though she was just delivering a message from the manager.

"Well, even so, you need to take some time out, we'll be in touch with you to book you in again at some point."

And that was that. I'd just increased my outgoings with the car and a new home, and my biggest source of income had gone down the pan.

Thank goodness I still had the agency. And worst-case scenario, I could always give myself dancing shifts. Plus Christmas was coming, and pubs and clubs always booked extra nights. People knew people, passed on my contact number and would ask me when I turned up to venues to collect the house fees if I could provide girls for x/y/z events. I still controlled all the lap dance venues (all bar one) in the nearby town to me. They added "The Madam" to my list of nicknames when I turned up to collect my monies. But I was always the first girl to call if anyone needed dancers.

There was also a strip club forum online, which I would scour from time to time, as I had when I had begun dancing. A lot of positions there were abroad. I had heard some horror stories of friends who had danced in Greece before; the owners tried to keep them there and wouldn't give back their passports. I knew other girls who had made it their job to dance abroad more than they danced in England, really enjoyed it, and worked in some lovely places where they were looked after. I had briefly looked into it not long after I set up my agency, as I had heard Canada and Japan were great places to work, and the clubs took care of the girls, offering them great accommodation and transport to and from the clubs, but then the SARS virus came about, which panicked dancers and they didn't want to travel to any part of Asia or Canada (there had been outbreaks there).

So I began emailing clubs throughout Europe. When checking out sending girls abroad, I always asked questions thoroughly, so I could write a full itinerary down for the girls. I wanted no stone left unturned. I wanted the girls to enjoy their trips wherever they were going, I wanted them to earn money, and more importantly, to be safe. It wasn't as though I could come and pick them up if there was a problem. Dancing in the rest of Europe was a little different from over here. Nearly every club offered a basic daily salary. Most countries had clubs which prioritised girls trying to sell champagne before dances (called hostessing). The girls received commission on any champagne they sold; the bigger the bottle, the more money. For every dance a girl did, the club took 50%. It seemed a lot, but girls were still earning well. Accommodation was a minimal cost, something like 10 Euros per day, and usually free rides to and from work. If they worked over a certain length of time (dependent on the club – anything from two weeks to one month), the club paid for some or all of their flights.

Ireland at the time was a topless-only club setting and focused more on girls selling dances than champagne; they tried not to encourage the girls to consume alcohol. If a girl wanted a drink, they could have a "dancers' cocktail", which unbeknown to the customer, was a fancy soft drink charged at the same price as alcohol. The remaining clubs in Europe on my list were nude, and some allowed touching: some just above the waist, whilst others offered more – I avoided the latter as the girls on my agency books weren't interested.

I had periodically tried sending some girls to Ireland the first few months of starting the agency, but the clubs had made excuses not to send me my commission; saying the girls weren't good enough and weren't making enough money, when the reason they weren't making money was because the club was dead. Eventually I ended up getting a good contact on my books for Dublin, through a girl called Raven I'd danced with in my first club in Mayfair. When she'd had enough of dancing in London, she went to Ireland for a few months and danced in a club in a village outside of Dublin. Said village had a church, a shop, a pub…and a lap dancing club. Despite that, and despite villagers protesting every night the club was open by standing outside holding up placards reading "Lap dancers out," Raven said the club was steady, good money, and the dancers were treated well by the owners. In time, the villagers got what they wanted; the club closed and the owner moved on to open a club in the basement of a hotel in Dublin. The setup was great – the girls would stay in the hotel, so all they had to do was walk downstairs to the venue.

I flew over to work a long weekend and took Claire with me. That way I could check out the venue, work it myself and report back to the girls. Claire and I shared a triple bedded room with another girl who was starting the same day as us and intended to stay longer. During the days we could come and go as we pleased and at 7pm we'd head down to work, finishing at 2am. The club wasn't all that big, and like the clubs in London, it never really got busy until after 10pm. Oddly enough, most of the guys were English, either over for stag dos or rugby. Unlike the clubs in London or Kent, almost every guy who set foot in this club committed to at least one dance. And the club was topless only (with a discretionary flash if they paid well), so they were in effect getting less than they would in England. Customers could also opt for a group show, whereby a group would come into the lap dance room and watch two girls perform a (topless) lesbian act in the middle of the room, with the occasional lap dancing bit in between. One night in particular, I, a blonde, was picked by a group of lads to do a lesbian show with an Irish girl, a brunette called Star. There were only two Irish girls working the club; most were from Eastern Europe.

Star and I agreed on a price and took the guys to the cashier. We never handled the money in this club. Guys paid the cashier, and we were handed tickets to put in our purse that were goods to the value of each dance. Cashing up was at the end of the following night; we received our money in envelopes, with a calculation including the number of dances and piccolos (dancers' cocktails), less the club's commission, written on the front. We led 6 of them to the room, I walked through and Star stood at the doorway, holding back the beaded curtain, allowing the men to follow me in.

"Take a seat, boys." I indicated, "Spread out a little so you have some room."

The room was rectangular, with bench seating around the perimeter. The space in the middle was around 6 feet by 8. We began dancing opposite ends of the room to give the guys a bit of up close and personal, and when we met in the middle we stepped back, so they could all see us easily, without having to lean over each other. Star began to kiss me and lower the top half of my dress down to my waist. I did the same to her as she groped my boobs. The guys watched in silence. Moving closer to them, I sat back on one of the customers and lap danced for him whilst Star leant towards me and sucked on my nipples. Then we swapped, she moved onto another guy and I leant down, kissing her neck, her lips and her boobs. We repeated it again…and then she bit me. She bit my fucking nipple. Now, my nipples are *extremely* sensitive, *ridiculously* sensitive. And I know some girls have trouble, but I have been blessed with being able to reach orgasm several ways, and through my nipples is one of them *if* the right person spends enough time on them (a little bit of trivia here for you – having your nipples played with correctly can result in the genital sensory cortex being stimulated, in the same way as the clitoris, vagina and cervix can stimulate it). Needless to say, nibbling or biting does *not* do it for me, in any way, shape or form.

"Oww, that bloody hurt!" I couldn't refrain from blurting something out as I definitely didn't want her biting me again.

"You don't like that?" she said, in front of the guys.

"Not particularly!"

We laughed it off because after all, these guys were paying to see us "enjoy" ourselves. We continued, taking it in turns to pay the guys attention and then back to us for girl-on-girl action. I was on my knees in between one of the guy's legs, with my boobs near their crotch area when Star took that as an invitation to get behind me on her knees and stroke my back and kiss my butt. The next minute, she gave me the biggest spank on my butt cheek and the guys went "Ooh!" as the spank echoed around the room. I thought:

"I can't moan at her again or they won't have any more dances."

So I put on a smile. It wasn't as unbearable as the nipple bite.

"Oh, ya like that don't cha?" She asked rhetorically in her hot Irish accent.

I wasn't sure whether she was addressing me or the guys, as they were nodding in answer. So we moved away from them, with me on my hands and knees and she continued to spank me a couple more times. Then she bent over, inviting me to do the same. Payback. I spanked her hard, and she let out a loud

"Ah yeah! That's it! Do it *hard*!"

It turned into a contest. She spanked, I spanked, she spanked; whether we were kneeling on the floor or draped over one of the customers, we each took it in turns to serve, with each of us looking to be the champion as to who could spank the hardest and loudest. When their time was up, our customers left the room, all smiling and laughing. As we got dressed, she apologised for biting my nipple:

"I thought you'd like it, cos I love tha' kinda thing"

"Nope unfortunately not, *or* hard spanking."

"Ah sorry, I'll know for next time."

Luckily there wasn't a next time with Star, but I learned another valuable lesson that night: if you're going to do a lesbian show with a girl you don't know very well and who doesn't know you, discuss do's and don'ts beforehand - one to avoid embarrassment and two, because if you work well together you can make the dance look even hotter, instead of gritting your teeth and your eyeballs nearly popping out of your head.

Despite a stinging ass and a sore nipple, the Dublin trip wasn't bad and Claire and I returned with decent money. A few of my dancers booked contracts there and enjoyed it. I trained one girl up from scratch and she asked to go to Dublin for her first job. She stayed there happily for 6 months, then moved on to a contract I had gained in the heart of Amsterdam, then back to Dublin until she quit dancing a year later.

Upon my return to England it was time to get ready for the crazy Christmas rush, as an agent and as a dancer.

15
THE MOST WONDERFUL
TIME OF THE YEAR

Ah, Christmas! Time for a dancing frenzy: single shifts, double shifts, triple shifts. If there are enough hours in the day to work, we'd still take the shift. Even on Christmas Eve.

"I can sleep on Christmas Day" was my motto.

The Christmas party season and the seasonal increase of money back in the early 2000s always started mid-November. Working on my own bookings was an advantage and if anyone heard of any others being run by friends or other agencies, we'd work those shifts too. A nightclub owner had heard of my agency and called to ask if I could provide him with four girls for a three-hour private afternoon event for his friend's Christmas party. They had all been out for a Christmas meal and drinks, so by the time we arrived, they were warmed up and ready to see naked girls. There were probably 50 guys. There was no stage, so we used the whole floor for our jug collection shows. I went first. I always thought this was the best move when we had a new venue, as I could explain the purpose of the jug to the guys if they didn't know what it was for. This time, even with an explanation it was still a mission. When it comes to a couple of guys within the same group deciding not to contribute, unfortunately this can lead to others following suit, like Disciples of the Dickheads, and it can make things pretty difficult. No one was putting in and after a few Nos I found the boss man for the night, who re-explained the rules, as if I had been speaking Martian. Then they were as good as gold until we'd all done one jug collection each. We asked if anyone wanted lap dances and all we kept getting was "maybe later". I told the girls we'd leave in another half hour if this continued, and I informed the owner politely what our plans were.

The fear of loss always provides a motivation to purchase. It's a worldwide sales tactic and it works in dancing too. You could be in the skimpiest of dancing clothes all night and no one has had a dance, but the minute they see you go to get changed, or even *get* changed and are about to leave, oftentimes, there will always be at least one customer who says:

"Oh, are you leaving? I wanted to get a dance."

It can be ridiculously annoying, especially if you've had a quiet night and have mentally transferred from "work mode" to "sod this, I'm going home" mode.

Lo and behold, after about 10 minutes, the boss and three of his friends wanted dances. We took them upstairs (three flights up) to what was usually the VIP room in the evenings and sat the guys on the sofas to begin our dance. They had the choice of four women: one blonde, one brunette, one with black hair and a redhead, the perfect mix. We hoped, after doing our first lap dances of the night, and especially one of them being for the manager too, that we would get more. There can be a tendency in humans to look at others' behaviour and do what's popular. Tonight they all decided to follow the leader. All four guys were happy with their dances and as they got up at the end of the dance to leave and we were putting our outfits back on, the boss overheard us chatting to each other, saying something along the lines of us needing to watch the stairs in our heels.

> "Well I have an idea about that," he said. "Come back down with me and I'll sort something."

Downstairs we faced the crowd of wide-eyed men wondering "what *really* went on upstairs?" and "how good was it?!"

The boss handed me one of the club's two-way radios for security staff.

> "Take that up with you and radio down to this guy (he pointed to a bouncer) when you're ready to have guys sent up."

He showed me which buttons to press and we tested it out before us girls went back upstairs, taking four new customers up with us. Once we were back in that room we didn't need to return downstairs. We took it in turns to use the radio as we thought the whole situation was comical and brilliant, taking laziness on our part to a whole new level.

> "We're ready for the next four, over…"

and like magic, new guys appeared. At no point were any of us without a dance as there were always four guys coming up at a time and at times they would stay for another dance and just ask us to swap over, which saved them trekking up the stairs again later.

No small talk, no putting yourself on parade for everyone to see in the hope they liked us. Just being put in a separate room, with a radio for giving orders. Great money - equal money between us, with no competing. Now if only every venue was like this – what a system! The guys had had a great day celebrating with mates over dinner, drinks and naked women and they didn't feel pressured. All they felt was perhaps a little out of breath from the three flights of stairs.

But like Yin and Yang, with ease comes difficulty. And my next job ended up being a pain in the ass (well, in my back actually) …

16
CHILLED TO THE BONE

One of the agents I worked for hired me to do some outdoor pole dance poses in London on a cold November morning, for a drinks company and Sunday supplement magazine. Naturally, I said yes; who doesn't want to be underdressed in the winter? Upon arrival I was given a red bikini – sporting the drinks brand logo on the side – which I paired up with my red knee-high platform boots and a long trench coat to protect me from the elements when walking the streets with the camera crew, agent, reporters and the head of the drinks company campaign. The trench coat only had two buttons, so failed to stop the cold wind blowing up inside it. I was booked for three hours, although I wasn't outside all that time. Our entourage walked through drizzling rain to Piccadilly Circus with someone holding an umbrella over me to prevent my hair and make-up getting spoiled.

People on the street stopped and watched us walk by; I looked like a celebrity. The reporters wanted me to pose on a lamppost in the middle of Piccadilly Circus, with Anteros, the naked statue at the top of the fountain, in the background. Once we arrived at the destination, however, they realised this wouldn't work, as the lampposts were not only too large, but also square at the bottom (not your average small-town lamppost that most drunkards throw themselves around and pretend to pole dance against at the end of a night out).

So now we were drawing attention to ourselves, with people wondering what we're doing, when in fact we were none the wiser either. The photographers gazed around, trying to work out the next move.

"Over there!" An excited reporter pointed to a building being renovated with scaffold poles outside. Plan B was decided.

After crossing the road and the photographers working out which angle had the better light, it was time to disrobe and wrap myself around the pole. Buses drove by tooting their horns and builders in white vans catcalled through their windows, goading me.

The reporter wanted to be in the picture:

>"Let's get this over with," he said as he took his jacket off, to wear just his t-shirt and jeans "it's cold and miserable out here."

>"*You're* moaning about the cold!?" I retorted "You're not the one wearing a bikini!"

He grabbed the same pole on the opposite side to me and crouched to come down to my height (I was about five feet seven in my boots), whilst I then wrapped my leg around him and held onto the pole. A few more snaps and we were done, heading back to the office, which couldn't happen soon enough.

With a warm coffee in hand and back into my jeans and sweater, I sat with my agent waiting for my pay. The company organiser walked over to hand her the money.

>"There you go, thank you so much," and smiled.

We both looked at the money, looked at each other, then looked back at her.

>"That's the amount we agreed to, right?" The assistant asked

"No, what you've given me here is an hourly rate, and Holly's worked three hours for you."

"Oh, sorry we were mistaken, we thought that price was for the whole three hours. And that was our budget." She shrugged her shoulders. "Here, have some complimentary drinks." And handed us three miniature bottles each, as if that was an adequate enough substitute for my pay.

I wasn't happy and neither was my agent as she worked on a percentage of my fee. The agreement was verbal, so we were stuck. If I had been the agent for this project, I would have made sure something was in writing. I always looked after "my girls" and everyone knew it. I was extremely pissed off to say the least, and to top it all I developed some kind of chill or cold which gave me terrible pain in my lower back due to being scantily clad on such a damp, cold day, and with it being near Christmas it was impossible to take any time off.

But being outdoors in a bikini was just the tip of the iceberg this year. And something deep in my psyche must have attracted this "be at one with the elements" circumstances, because lo and behold, the newspaper group were now running a magazine and they called me up:

"Hey Holly, we're doing a naked locations piece called "Flashing in the Street" and wondered if you'd be interested? You'll be posing in your home town or county."

"Who thinks of these things!?" I thought. (Obviously a male of the species).

But I never turned down any work, especially not from the company that paid me well when they offered me some.

The photographer picked me up on a cold, frosty morning. There was another model working on the project, so she and I could alternate getting out of the car and flashing from coats, which was good as one of us could keep warm whilst the other one was doing the hard work. The photographer drove around aimlessly until he'd find somewhere or something he liked the look of for us to pose in front of. "Welcome to…" road signs, milestones, the outside of historic buildings, monuments and statues of famous people; no landmark was safe from our naked flesh. Smiling in the cold weather, trying to look like it was no big deal being naked in public and then keeping our wits about us, ready to close our coats or run back to the car if anyone cottoned on to what we were doing, was pretty arduous. The last thing we wanted was to get arrested for indecent exposure. I thought of the bikini shoot against the scaffolding the couple of weeks before and laughed at how I'd thought that was a cold day. But *now,* here I was, wearing nothing but a smile and a pair of black knee boots, straddled across a cannon on a hill, with a statue of Lord Kitchener standing watch.

I remembered Kitchener's poster slogan:

"Your Country Needs You."

Yes, yes it does;

"It needs you to put some bloody clothes on, woman!"

Whereas Anteros, the Greek God of requited love probably wouldn't have minded me posing near him, what I was doing now just wasn't "very British" and I'm pretty sure the old Field Marshall wouldn't have approved. I wasn't just getting a cold in my back right now. The icy metal cannon shot pain in between my legs until my pubic bone and all around it went numb. The metal chains Lydia and I pressed against our bodies in the ironmonger's factory visit months before had nothing on this – at least the bottom halves of our bodies were covered up and we were indoors. It's funny how you think you'll never get another shoot that's any more uncomfortable than the one you're currently doing.

It was a blessing that the frost had cleared. Visions of my vagina and thighs being frozen to the large black artillery ran through my head, along with all the "how would I get off?" scenarios…would the other model have to run over to the petrol station across the road and ask them to warm up a kettle of water? Or would I have to wait for the sun to thaw me out? *Or* would we have to go get members of the military at the barracks up the road to save me? Wow, my mind would run amok sometimes.

"I'd prefer to do this next time in the summer, if there is a next time" I said to the photographer.

I was pretty sure overall my skin would look better in the photos without goosebumps.

"Well, it's whenever the paper thinks about it, but when the weather warms up give them a call and put the idea in their head. We'll never run out of places to shoot, Kent has a lot of historic landmarks."

That it does. And lo and behold, when I was dancing in one of my pubs one Friday afternoon, a couple of builders told me about a new site they were working on.

"We buried a time capsule there and one of the things we put in it was a picture of you from a magazine where you're flashing in the street. We thought it was apt seeing as you're local" they said, smiling with excitement.

They could have put anything in that time capsule. Something sentimental, something that would be historic of the noughties in the years to come. But no, they chose to put in a naked photo of Holly Burnett. So, one day in the future, when I'm either really old or really dead, some poor bugger is going to open that up and see my tits and arse and wonder if that's how, as tourists, we posed in front of landmarks on a splendid day out.

God help us all.

17
OPEN WIDE

Andy, the photographer that always shot me for the newspaper group, also worked for one of the men's top-shelf magazines that shot American open leg style pictures – full nudity but more graphic than the work I had done for him previously, in that you held your vagina open. They were called "top-shelf magazines" because that's where newsagents kept them – far out of reach of children. Men would buy a newspaper and pop the magazine inside so other people in the queue wouldn't see. A bright idea for the Newsagents really, as they would end up selling an extra newspaper, and a clever disguise for lascivious content.

Andy knew I hadn't modelled for any American level shoots before so wanted his publication to be the first to put me in and asked if I'd travel to his studio in Manchester. I felt comfortable around him as he never acted like a pervert; all he was interested in was taking good pictures and getting paid. I'd staggered the levels I'd worked up to over the past year and a half, and other than the newspaper group there weren't many publications that worked below American level. For the few that did, they still only sought models that had something – namely a specific feature like really big boobs or who were naturally perfect in every way. Seeing as I looked more "girl next door", with naturally ok sized boobs (30D), and a UK size 10 body, I was never going to be photographed by those publications, so felt ready to work up to the next level for Andy and his. I probably wouldn't have said yes to another photographer.

Andy's place was a flat above a shop, converted into a photography studio. There was a canopy bed, a sofa, a desk and enough room for floor work on a cream fluffy carpet, which is where Andy decided to shoot me.

I'd taken up my stripper case full of clothes and shoes, not knowing what he was going to want me to wear, but he wanted a sluttier look and searched through his boxes of clothes which were all marked up according to dress sizes. I put on my make-up whilst he was talking to himself and rummaging. He'd pull out a dress, held it up to look at it, looked at me and then put it back in disagreement with himself. Head back in the box, concentrating:

> "Do your makeup darker, it needs to look a lot darker." He said, yet I didn't think he had noticed whilst he was so fixated in his container of clothes.

His eyes were everywhere. I'd already made it pretty heavy, anymore and I'd look like a gothic drag queen. But he insisted "the darker the better" and I guess he knew the look the magazine wanted, and how the pictures would come out.

> "Found it" – as he held up a red leather skirt with buckles all at the sides, "I want you to put this on, with this bra, and…" his eyes glazed over a pile of assorted hosiery, all in packets, before tossing each pack to the side by lightly skimming them with his fingertips, like a poker dealer would a pack of cards "…these fish nets. What size shoe are you?"

> "Four" I replied.

He picked out a red pair the same shade as the skirt, with an ankle buckle, a deadly point at the toes and a silver spiked heel, and handed me the complete outfit.

Open Wide

The fishnets were cream crotchless tights. Sporting a whole red leather and cream number, along with heavy black eye makeup and bright red lipstick, I no longer looked like a model. I looked like a girl who was about to be sent to the nearest street corner to make £20 a pop giving hand jobs in the passenger seat of a hatchback. Nevertheless, I was getting paid for "a look" that fitted the magazine, so it wasn't really up to me.

Andy worked me hard. And if he needed me to arch my back more when I was bent over, or stretch my leg out to a slightly different angle, he would be more hands-on and move my leg himself or press my back more. Usually photographers weren't supposed to touch us at all. But it was Andy. I didn't ever feel worried around him or that he had some sort of ulterior motive because he never did. He was totally professional – he didn't try to "accidentally" put a hand somewhere he shouldn't. Little did I know then that taking photos with him was unlike any other shoot I'd ever done; him bending me and stretching me about would feel like the equivalent of having a full-on work out and nothing would prepare me for the way I was going to ache the next day.

It was strange putting my fingertips either side of my pussy lips and holding them apart, whilst I had my legs mostly at the position of 2.10 (if you imagine my legs were clock hands). Strange also because of the facial expressions I had to pull whilst I posed that way. Now the sultry, screw your nose up, open your mouth and tip your head back, look like you're about to orgasm pose, was understandable. But the smile lots and look like "I'm so happy to be here, with my super open vagina, welcome everybody!" look just didn't do it for me and I wondered how any man would even get off on that. But again, Andy knew what he was doing as he'd been selling photos to the same magazine company for years.

I figured this was something I didn't ever need to tell my Granddad about, as he never bought top shelf mags. He knew I danced naked, had worked on the TV and was a topless model for the paper. He didn't really need to know the rest. He used to say to me:

> "Don't ever take this too far, or you'll never get yourself a decent boyfriend and no one will want you."

Pretty direct, but he always was. That's probably why I've always been so direct too – always telling it like it is. He was implying porn, and I'm guessing full on boy-girl porn. Granddad would reiterate those words to me time and time again. He knew some of the girls I worked and associated myself with did that job and I guess he didn't want me to be "led astray," but I told him I had no intention of doing it. All he could do was trust in me that I wouldn't let him down. Lying on my back, touching my nether regions in a pair of crotchless tights and red heels was nothing close to being rammed by a guy on camera, but even so if Granddad knew I'd gone a step further, it would just create more anguish for him. He was taking enough medication with his giant cell arteritis and through careful moderation it was currently under control. Stress can do strange things to the body and I wasn't going to risk that by telling Granddad I was posing for men's magazines.

When my photos came out in next month's magazine issue, they looked amazing. I looked amazing. My dark makeup didn't look anywhere near as dark as it had in reality, nor did the hideous outfit Andy had made me wear evoke that I was a hooker. Slutty yes, but not a whore. I was the double-page spread – literally, with my orgasm face, "Holly" written beside my head and the text "rip my stockings and fuck me" next to my legs. Andy and the publishers had made me the pull-out poster girl; I was a centrefold like the J. Geils Band had once sung about. Although I'd no idea who would stick a photo of me with my privates out on their wall and perhaps it was best that I didn't.

Now that I had the experience of one magazine, I looked again in *The Stage* newspaper under the modelling section to see if there were any jobs going that I could apply for – and any photographers I could possibly offer my agency services to. I emailed all potential opportunities with my résumé, one full length topless picture and a headshot photo. I received a call from an agent called Rachel:

"Hi Holly, I see you've worked up to American level in publications, and you did a bit of webcam some time ago; how would you feel about starring in a girl-girl film?"

18

GIRL ON GIRL

The girl-girl webcam that I'd previously done with Lydia was shot not only at a distance, but from the side so there were no close ups or views of insertion, and a lot of the time we just made out we were putting in toys or fingers whilst our legs blocked the views. The pixels from the webcam probably weren't all that great either.

I'd only just got used to up-close camera work for publication with Andy, but did I want close-ups of my genitalia on video? More to the point, did I want to be filmed having sex with a girl? And with a girl I'd never met before? I mean, what if there was no chemistry? Surely it would look crap on film? And not forgetting, this was for an adult TV channel. I was already known on the babe channels, so my face would be easily recognisable. This film, however, was for a larger company than I'd worked with before; a multi-media entertainment conglomerate, established in the US, that did TV, magazines and DVDs. If I agreed to this, I'd be a hardcore girl-girl porn star. Hardcore meant insertion – you didn't have to fuck a guy. The minute you stuck a toy in you, you were doing "hardcore."

I needed time to think but it wasn't a firm no, which surprised me. I told Rachel I would call her back the following day with an answer. The words that Granddad drummed in me about not being able to get a boyfriend ran around my head, but I wasn't going to be having sex with a man on camera and surely it wouldn't affect me in later relationships as most men fantasised about women getting off with each other. Many a time guys I danced for at work would go weak at the knees for two girls dancing for them at the same time (we called these double dances). And now for the (ever so slightly) scientific part as to why men like the idea of two women at it:

Neuroscience suggests that men are more sensitive to visual cues than women are. Doubling up visual stimuli (in this case, two women rather than just one) makes men even more aroused. The Amygdala in the limbic system of the brain plays a role in sexual activity and libido as it gauges emotional content, and is usually slightly bigger in males, which could explain why women are less into visual sexual cues rather than descriptive ones. The non-scientific reasoning could also be that men's sapphic preference is due to thinking that two girls becoming a threesome with the spectator (i.e., the man) is a huge turn on for them. However, if they watched a three way in porn (two girls, one man) it wouldn't be the same as they imagine themselves being there less since there's already a guy in the picture.

Knowing the film was for such a high-grade company, I guessed that the girl starring with me would be fairly pretty. And I was also sure that she would probably have more experience than me, so worst case scenario, she could take the lead. I doubted they would hire two novices.

There were still certain rules for what was allowed to be shown on TV in the UK, even on pay-per-view. They couldn't show anything too up-close, nor could they show insertion. Even for boy-girl, they weren't allowed to show a full erection; once it reached an angle of 90 degrees, they couldn't show the penis getting any harder. Rawer footage was saved for DVD sales. I discovered later that this is why the filming took longer – so they could get softer angles for TV, and harder angles for retail.

I called Rachel.

"Okay, I'll do it."

"Great" she replied. "Well it's next week so you'll have to go into London to get your STI checks done so they can give you a certificate on the same day."

It was compulsory in the industry for anyone doing hardcore to get their STI (Sexually Transmitted Infection) tests done and they had to be 28 days in date. If I went to a good old NHS hospital, it would take up to two weeks and they wouldn't give you a printed certificate. I found a private practice near Victoria station and booked in my test a few days before the shoot. It didn't particularly faze me, as I'd been tested a couple of times before. The first time was the worst, which was after I'd been raped all those years ago. I was younger, more naïve and cried all the way through it, albeit being a month or so after it had happened as I couldn't bring myself to go to the hospital any sooner and feel violated again like I had been that night. I didn't tell the nurses why I was there – what had happened. So when I panicked they just assumed I was being a drama queen, rather than the real reason. If I had plucked up the courage to tell them, then maybe they wouldn't have held me down to do the test like they did, which obviously made me feel a damn sight worse. I trembled for the rest of the day as memories of my ordeal flooded back to me. Bedside manners had since improved over time and I never experienced anything like that again, and this time, paying to get your tests done to get a certificate meant there was an even better level of customer service.

There was a big difference, modelling for such a premium company. I was to turn up with no makeup on because they provided a makeup artist, which was great especially if we had to be on set super early. With most shoots for smaller companies, especially early morning ones, I'd have most of my makeup on before I arrived – which meant getting up at the crack of dawn – because you never knew if you'd be stuck in traffic and get there late and applying a full face of makeup would then eat into the photographer's time. Some sets you worked on were only booked for a certain amount of time, or they may have had another model in after you and being punctual always meant there was a better chance they would book you again.

I arrived at the location, a detached house in Surrey, at around 9am, with my stripper case full of clothes. I had no idea what they'd want me to wear so I brought a selection of underwear sets, skirts, tops and a couple of different pairs of heels. I knocked on the solid wooden door and a blonde girl opened it with a friendly smile.

"Hiya, I'm Crystal, what's your name?"

"Holly," I said as I walked through the door and shook her hand.

"Oh, you're the model I'm working with today. Have you done much work before?"

She sat down on a chair where she continued to have her makeup applied by the makeup artist, who nodded at me in acknowledgement.

"Well I've done a bit of webcam and some magazine work, but other than that not really. This is my first hardcore film."

I tried not to appear too embarrassed by my lack of experience and continued the conversation.

"How about you?"

"Well I've done a fair bit of girl-girl stuff and solo. Mainly for amateurs, as there always seems to be a lot more of that about, but when these shoots come up, you've got to make the most of them."

I nodded in agreement, as I laid out my clothes on the large sofa so they wouldn't be crumpled in my case.

"You'll be fine, don't worry!" she said.

Was it that obvious I was nervous? Crystal was pretty, she had piercing blue eyes, was a little taller than me and her body was a similar size. I was surprised they booked two girls on a shoot that looked so similar to be honest. Usually in porn they have contrasting girls – different hair styles, or one with big boobs, one with small boobs. The main difference was her hair was shorter than mine – she had a bob.

The scene was to be filmed in the kitchen. It was decked out country-style, with antique white cupboard doors and oak coloured worktops, an oak dining table and eight matching chairs. There were two cameramen.

After our makeup was done and we were both dressed – wearing short skirts and skimpy tops with our matching knicker and bra sets, we walked into the kitchen and sat by the dining table to start on the stills, which always took precedence over video because the makeup was fresh and perfect.

Crystal and I began to kiss slowly and stop mid tongue in mouth so there was no blurring in the photos. To be fair, doing the stills first made me feel more comfortable. Not only was I used to doing them, it meant she and I could get acquainted easier, rather than getting straight to it. She smiled as she stuck her tongue in her mouth and I responded back. She was a pretty good kisser. We slowly stripped each other off. I pulled her top off and she did the same to me. She dropped both straps of my bra and unfastened it and it fell to the floor as she paid attention to licking one nipple, then the other. I stroked her hair and looked down at her with a smirk whilst we stopped and started for the camera. The cameraman asked us to speed up a bit as we seemed to forget we were supposed to be taking direction. We definitely had chemistry. He gave us instructions for the next couple of photos. One of me perching on the edge of the table, Crystal crouching down by my pussy and putting a couple of centimetres of my toy in me, and another of me on my knees in between Crystal's legs, whilst she sat on one of the chairs.

"Okay, thanks," said the photographer, "now put your clothes back on and we'll start filming."

The makeup artist entered the kitchen to readjust our hair and touch up our lipstick for continuity. There wasn't really any dialogue or storyline to the film, thank goodness, because I wasn't sure I'd be particularly ready for any acting and would probably have forgotten the lines due to nerves. I just had to act like I was into women; truth be told I was getting there, and I definitely fancied Crystal.

This time, without direction, we began the film with lots of kissing whilst grabbing each other's hair and taking off each other's clothes. Crystal was right, she *was* experienced, and I wondered if I was doing a good enough job for a "proper" film. I had nothing to compare it to. I knew that I wasn't bad in the bedroom department as men always came back, but all I could do was continue the scene and hope for the best. And whether she was faking or not, the job wasn't about enjoying yourself, it was about money for us. Although if the magnetic attraction looked good on camera, the whole film would look better.

As we stood in front of the table, I crouched down and removed Crystal's thong. She sat on the edge of the chair and opened her legs for me whilst I got on my knees in front of her. I licked my middle finger and slid it inside her, moving my hand back and forth, and then moved my face lower so I could lick her clitoris at the same time. Crystal breathed deeper than she had been, but I couldn't stay in this position too long as my head was blocking the close-ups of the camera. Everything had to be done at an angle, rather than how you would "perform" in the bedroom normally, so instead of me being full face down, I had to tilt my head to the side as I stuck out my tongue. It was too awkward that way, so I concentrated on fingering Crystal instead and pushed another digit inside of her, whilst I moved my arm back and forth, increasing the speed as she writhed on the chair, moaning and smiling. She was close. I went faster, as fast as I could and her muscles tightened up around my fingers, so I knew she wasn't faking it. Once her body relaxed again, I stood up and leaned towards her and she kissed me with gratitude.

"Your turn," she said quietly to me, with a glint in her eye.

I laid back on the table and she pushed my legs up in the air and lifted my hips to remove my thong. I bent my legs so my feet were on the edge, either side of her head. Crystal licked me, from my clit to the entrance to my vagina and back again. When she decided I was wet enough, she lightly placed two fingertips on and around my clit and moved them in light circular motions to tease me and prep me for what was next. She reached for the vibrator and switched it on. I sat up on my elbows, watching her. With a hand on one of my thighs to hold me steady she guided the vibrator into me, as far as it would go, and then pulled it out, leaving all but one inch inside me. I pushed against it, demanding more and she continued to fuck me with it, whilst one cameraman stayed down that end and the other one filmed my top half for close-up facial expressions of rapture and bouncing boob shots. I laid back down and put my arms out to the side, holding on to the table to move back and forth as she fucked me rapidly until my cheeks flushed and I felt myself coming intensely. My legs shook and she removed the toy as the cameraman was doing a close up in between my legs. I didn't just come; I creamed. A lot. I guess Crystal wanted to prove she could do the same to me as I had to her. She put the toy down and held my pussy lips apart so the cameraman could see it all.

"That's great" he said, "now squeeze her lips together and then open them again."

Crystal did as he said. More cream came out.

"The men are going to love this" he uttered, fascinated.

I guess not every girl did what I managed to do – what Crystal had made me do. She did it for a few more seconds until we heard the word "Cut".

"Well done, girls. We've got enough footage now."

They put both cameras down and we picked up our clothes and went and got changed.

"Do you feel better now you've done your first girl-girl film?" Crystal asked.

I was smiling a lot:

"Yeah, I don't know why I felt so nervous, it was easier than I thought it would be. And fun!"

As I packed up my bag and signed the model release form (a legal document to allow the company to publish the pictures and film – every company wanting to publish had to get a model to fill one out by law), I switched on my phone and it pinged with messages from friends asking how it went. I felt like I had conquered something amazing. But all I had done was fuck a girl on camera. And thank goodness she was pretty so I could tell the tale. As I was about to leave, Crystal gave me a piece of paper.

"Here's my number. Call me and I'll give you some contacts for more work if you want."

"Thank you so much!" I said gratefully.

"No problem."

She leaned in to kiss me goodbye. This time without cameras.

"I'm always happy to help, and I'd really like to see you again…"

19
TIME TO PLAY

Between Christmas and New Year I desperately needed to let my hair down: all work and no play was making Holly a dull girl.

People outside of the "adult entertainment industry" thought we partied all the time, but work for me, although sociable, wasn't a party. You need separation, you need to go out and socialise when you're not at work. To wear what you want, to talk to who you choose to and to meet people and hang out without feeling the need to earn money. So I went out clubbing with friends I'd not been out with in a long time. We drank, we talked, we danced on the dancefloor (but not as much as I used to – now I danced for a living, dancing on my day off, even though it was a different type of dancing altogether, seemed more like a chore). One of my friends, who I had text to come out earlier on in the night, Greg, didn't reply back to me until later:

"Sorry I couldn't make it, was out with family. Are you still out?"

I texted back.

"Yes! Come down!"

Not realising there was only half an hour until the club was going to close. I love those nights – when you're having such a good time it doesn't seem like it's the end of the night.

"Come get a cab to mine and we can catch up."

"Catch up" at 2am. Instant booty call. But being the drunk, horny, "I need to let my hair down" girl I was that night, I hopped into a cab straight to his (mum's) house.

Greg was waiting by the front door so I wouldn't knock or ring the bell and he signalled for me to go up the stairs. Obviously I was right – he was thinking the same as me. There were no crossed wires here.

214

Booty call. I'd been with him a couple of times in the past when he lived in Bristol and I'd visited him, before I was with Josh (oddly enough they used to go to school together), but I actually met Greg in another night club during my first few months of stripping, when I was proud of telling everyone:

"I'm a lap dancer."

He didn't believe me, so he got a free "clothed" dance in the club, just so he could see my moves. We exchanged numbers, although I couldn't remember his name, so I punched him in my phone book as "Man" and when he finally texted me two days later, a "who's this?" reply got me his name.

So with his mum asleep in the other room, we had to be as quiet as we could and I crept up the stairs, still wearing my thigh-high boots. Trying to take them off downstairs and drunk would probably have resulted in me stumbling, falling and waking her up. Also when I'm drunk I have no idea whether I'm being quiet.

Once in his room, we got straight to it. We kissed, then I sat on the edge of the bed and he proceeded to go down on me whilst I still had my (very short) skirt on. He lifted my legs up to pull my thong off and then held onto my hips to pull me further towards him and keep me firmly in place so that I wouldn't wriggle away. I kept my legs up, knees bent and ankles crossed and rested on his back. I was still wearing my boots. Maybe this was intentional, maybe I was living out Greg's fantasy – a girl in thigh boots. I'm pretty sure his exes never dressed like this.

I pulled his head up to kiss me and taste myself on his lips. Then I undid his belt whilst he unzipped the fly of his jeans and I reached into his boxers for his already hard cock. I flicked my tongue around the glans and only took half of him in my mouth before he said he needed to lay down or his legs would turn to jelly and he'd fall to the floor. Once he laid down, I continued to suck him, to lick him, to take all of him in my mouth whilst I held onto the base with my hand. When he was ready, I rose up from between his legs and straddled him. With the tip of his cock right at the entrance of my pussy, I stopped, staring at him, with a glimmer in my eye. Being drunk I developed, what I thought was either Dutch courage or sexual spontaneity to make myself appear more attractive to him

"You're okay, I know you and you're my mate, you won't have anything..."

And with that I slid slowly down on his cock, bareback, and rode him like there was no tomorrow…

…and that, my friends, is how sexual spontaneity has consequences, and how I caught chlamydia.

20
ASSHOLE AGENTS

How did I find out about the chlamydia? I went to get tested for work again, but this time I was in America.

Rachel had sent me over there with five other people who wanted to get into the porn industry in the USA. I told her I was only going to do girl-girl if anything came up and I would mainly dance. The majority of people, including girls who worked for me over here, filled me with rumours:

> "They're going to take your passport away and make you do films with men/ It'll be dangerous over there as you won't know anyone and you'll get into a predicament."

I wasn't stupid. I checked and double checked with Rachel before I booked my flight, telling her I didn't want to waste her time going over if the end game was to persuade me to do boy-girl and she assured me that wouldn't be the case and I would not be made to do something I didn't want to.

Out of the five I was to meet with, the two guys, Brandon and Jonathan, had worked in the industry before, but only in the UK. One of the girls, Scarlet, who was to meet us a few days later, had worked in the US for three months the year before and only worked in the US. Amber had never even danced, let alone modelled, although she was six feet one and slender so could have passed for a catwalk model. Tiffany had been an escort and wanted to try making more money doing porn.

We were to all meet in Vegas and spend around four days there for the AVN (Adult Video News) Adult Entertainment Expo. This was a yearly exhibition, where day fans could meet their favourite porn stars and get signed photos, see the newest films due out and buy merchandise. One night out of the four there was an awards ceremony, like the Oscars for adult films. Our agent planned to meet us all in Vegas, after which we would go and stay with her in Los Angeles for work.

Brandon, Jonathan and I flew from the UK to LA. For some strange reason and I've no idea why we agreed to do this the long way around (as Amber and Tiffany flew straight to Vegas), we were to meet Rachel's boyfriend at LAX airport. There was a black limo waiting to take us to Las Vegas. We were knackered, but driving through the desert and then finally seeing the bright lights of Vegas was something else. It was mesmerising.

24 hours door-to-door and we arrived at our hotel, where Tiffany and Amber were waiting in the lobby. When I had booked my flight, the hotel rooms were already sorted by one of the boys and all I had to do was pass the money over to him. But when Amber approached the front desk to check us all in, there was a problem with one of the rooms. The hotel realised that it was their mistake, so they had to upgrade us to a $600 per night suite, for 2 nights, with complimentary room service for that night to say sorry. It had gone midnight, but we were buzzing with excitement at our amazing suite on the 22nd floor. Fruit, toast, sweet breads, cereals, teas and alcohol were delivered to us and we tucked in. I didn't fancy any booze as it was technically breakfast time over in England. We all got to know each other whilst eating and drinking; about three of the party doing so by having a communal bath as the tub was huge. I declined and settled for a solo shower before trying to get some sleep.

I managed a little rest, but jetlag got the better of me – something I'd never dealt with before as I'd never travelled long haul. Looking out of our hotel window and seeing the Statue of Liberty was surreal. I knew very little about Vegas, but was sure the Statue of Liberty was in New York. It took a while for me to realise that most hotels out there were themed, so had no need to question my intelligence any longer.

I buddied up with Tiffany the next day to hang out and go to the convention. Porn stars galore stood at film production booths, in short skirts and booty shorts, low-cut tops and with faces full of professionally done makeup. I had never seen so many beautiful people in one room. I passed a stand that specifically filmed all-girl productions and spoke to the director.

"Oh, you're from England?" his interest in me broadened when he heard my accent.

"Yes, I'm over here for about three weeks, I'm leaving for LA in a few days."

"Well, we'd definitely be interested in shooting you…here's my card. Call me when you're in LA (the majority of producers at the AVN here were from LA) and we'll book you."

I took his card, and explained I'd speak to my US agent Ellen and get her to get in touch. Even though I found this job myself, I knew I couldn't bypass her as my agent and she would still want a cut. The deal was for us to pay rent at her house and 20% of the payment we earned from doing movies (dancing not included), 10% for Ellen, 10% for Rachel. And being an agent myself, I totally got it. In a way, I thought this would be great – showing initiative to Ellen. But when I met her later for the first time, she didn't seem at all bothered that I'd got the gig. In fact, she seemed pretty cold for someone who made a percentage out of people working for her. She hardly spoke to us and it almost felt like we were in her way most of the time, from meeting her in Vegas, to riding back with her to LA. She didn't even want to make conversation. Ellen did what she needed to for her own means only. She had no intention of getting to know any of us.

Once in LA, Koreatown to be exact, Ellen drove us girls around various film companies (Brandon and Jonathan had hired a car so they followed later), where they took Polaroids of us naked along with our body stats and what levels we would work up to. But the words:

"Oh, you *only* do girl-girl?" repeated on and on and on at me.

And I repeated:

"Yes, that's right, *just* up to girl-girl"

No one showed me any interest, but they did with the other girls, as they were new faces for their companies, and Scarlet who they all seemed to love, as she had shot some great content for them in the past, and went up to anal. One of the directors said to her:

"We're shooting a new extreme series, whereby girls put oversized dildos inside them – we're looking for someone who can use that…"

He pointed over to the corner of the room and there was a glass dildo, standing upright on the floor and must have been about 2 feet high and four or five inches in diameter.

I sat in silence, waiting for Scarlet to respond:

"I wouldn't be able to get that in my ass" she said, as she shook her head.

"Oh my God," I said, "I'm SO glad you just said that!"

I wasn't ready to be scarred by imagining someone I knew taking something so extreme in their orifice. A lot of the porn I'd watched in the past hadn't been that excessive, but now I was in Porn Valley, learning about more than I wanted to. I probably looked too much of an angel for these companies. After driving around to a few of them, Ellen took us to go get blood tests done for our Health Certificates. The turnover for results was 24 hours.

I'd picked up a couple of industry magazines whilst we were visiting the companies and as well as porn companies and agencies, there were lots of lap dancing clubs advertised. There were some that were clubs where you wore a bikini at all times, some where you wore pasties (patches to cover up your nipples), some were topless and some were nude. I circled a few and called around and Ellen said she would take me to audition at a couple of them in West Hollywood the next day.

That morning, we got our results. Ellen had been to pick them up and whilst she was driving a couple of other girls around she gave me a call:

> "As if things weren't going bad enough for you (I had no idea what she meant by that, other than I wasn't getting much interest in film work), you've got chlamydia."

I'd never caught anything in my life so I started to panic and hyperventilated. Turned out a course of antibiotics would sort it out (paid for, as of course, there was no National Health Service in

America), and in the meantime I needed to drop the bomb to Greg as he was the last person I'd slept with. I also called Crystal and she said she didn't have it as she'd just been retested for her certificates, so it had to have come from Greg. And he wasn't best pleased when I delivered the news, although it should have been me that was mad at him.

I got myself ready for my audition and Tiffany was having an early night as she had her first job booked the next day with two guys on a boat. She was nervous and didn't know what to expect so just wanted to try to sleep rather than overthink how it would go.

There were awkward silences in the car with Ellen. I thought now I'd been at hers for a couple of days things would be better, but she was still very standoffish. There was only so much I could say to her if she was being unresponsive.

We arrived at the first club. It was fairly small, with red lighting and purple drapes. There was a catwalk type stage in the middle of the floor and after talking to the manager he asked me to audition whilst the club was empty. I danced to whatever music happened to be playing and I got the job. He asked if I could start the next night and I said yes. *Finally* I would begin to have an income whilst being out there for the next couple of weeks, even if I didn't get much film work. We never went to any other clubs, I just went with the first yes and then we went back to Ellen's.

In the morning a very nervous Tiffany was driven to her job and then Ellen came back. She asked to see me in her office. I thought it was going to be about driving me to work that night.

She turned away from her computer and looked at me:

"I'm not going to be making enough money off you if you just dance" she said.

"But I'm going to be able to pay my rent after today."

Four of us were sleeping in one room in bunk beds and she was earning a fair amount from that.

"Well I need to be earning commission off you like I am the other girls. I can't get you any other girl-girl work, so you're going to have to do boy-girl."

I took one look at her and laughed a little under my breath:

"I don't *have* to do anything."

I don't know who she thought I was, but I wasn't someone who could be bullied into doing something I didn't want to do. And Rachel had told me this would not be the case.

"Well you're taking up space in my house when I could be earning more off another model, so you're going to have to move out when another one arrives."

"So can you hang on for a week until I start making some money from dancing so I can move out and find somewhere else to stay?" I asked.

"No" she said.

Just like that. A big fat, short no. I think she thought I was going to back down.

"Well in that case," I took a deep breath and sat back in my chair, "You and Rachel had better pay for my flight home, because otherwise I'm not going anywhere…"

21
BOLD BEHAVIOUR

Ellen informed Rachel I was coming back and managed to book me a flight for the next day, with half the money coming out of Rachel's pocket and half out of her own. Tiffany had also decided that porn wasn't for her and chose to fly home. Being in a movie wasn't how she'd imagined; she cried on and off all the way through the filming and when she got back to Ellen's. Escorting – sleeping with men behind closed doors for money – was more straightforward for her.

Once I was back in England, I didn't want to hear the "I told you so's," from everyone who'd warned me against going to the USA, so I laid low for about a week and continued to let Dee deal with the agency bookings. I had no work booked for myself for another three weeks so uploaded my details on a couple of model forums that Crystal had told me about. The forums were for amateur and professional modelling jobs, and just like the camera clubs and agencies I'd applied to before, there were boxes to tick to state your levels, but this time you could tick a higher level for amateur and a lower level for professional if you wanted to (some girls would choose to do more if it wasn't published compared to work that was). I ticked up to girl-girl on both, uploaded some photos and hit the submit button...

It didn't take long for messages to appear in my inbox. I guess the photographers received updates if new models in their area appeared on the site. But a lot of the messages I received were asking if I did boy-girl:

"It will only be with me whilst I film it"

"I won't publish it"

"It will be for my own "personal" use" (translated: "to wank over when I'm feeling fruity.")

I remained as polite as I could, explaining that I only went as high as I'd already stated on the forum.

"I'll pay you more"

"But you're so pretty"

"You'd do so well doing boy-girl" – translated: "you look like a good fuck to me and I want to do you."

One guy even asked if he could pose in some photos with me and I said yes up to topless, and then I received this message:

"Can I be nude if I put a condom on my dick, because then I'm still covered up?

No, no and NO! I had been on two forums for three hours and already it felt like I was back in LA being told I had no choice but to do boy-girl. But Crystal informed me that it happens to most new models who subscribe and a lot of photographers will try it on to see who's naïve and who's not. It's pretty awful really; that young models who weren't as level headed as me may end up getting in too deep before they realise that they are.

As luck would have it, a guy who shot professional photos for one of the men's magazines was one of the first "legit" photographers to contact me and asked me to do a solo (toy) shoot, with 2 dress changes. And I agreed he could shoot at my flat, seeing as it was huge and had lots of different rooms. Not only was the natural lighting pretty good but if photographers brought professional lighting my ceilings were high and the rooms were big enough to add softboxes (photographic devices that modified the light).

The shoot was to be more of a girl next door type – wearing a dress or short skirt and a top. The usual strip down, change expression, change positions and then stick a toy in you. Pretty straightforward for stills when I now had the experience. And working from home was great as I didn't have to think of what to pack in a suitcase.

We did the first set of photos at the dining room table and the second on my sofa. The guy made me feel pretty comfortable and we chatted as I posed and he shot the photos. We talked randomly about models we knew and photographers I'd worked with. I posed with my blue pearlescent vibrator, which was always my favourite – perhaps because it was the smoothest and looked good on camera, or maybe I was sentimental because it was the first vibrator I'd owned for work. It was a gift from one of the sex shops I worked in when I worked for the newspaper group. I put it down on the sofa as I finished the shoot and put a robe on. Whilst we talked, I noticed the photographer slowly move my vibrator along the sofa, just by a couple of inches, as if it was in his way, but he moved it from the end that I'd inserted into me. Then, whilst we were still talking, he put the two fingers that he'd moved the toy with, up to his nose and rubbed them around it. I didn't say anything, he thought I hadn't noticed, and what could I say really? He'd already done the deed and was sniffing his fingers. I couldn't believe his audacity. I didn't care that I thought initially he was great to work with; now, I couldn't wait for the covert pervert to leave. I wondered how often he was a toy sniffer, and how many models had noticed what I had, or whether his actions most of the time went unseen. Thankfully, not all togs were like that. Even though some try to get you to do a level further, or try to touch you, I never expected one of them to push the boundaries in such a peculiar way as this.

Then there were the nice photographers who shot a set of photographs, didn't even try to touch you and you had a laugh and a joke all the way through. I remember one guy specifically who shot for a men's magazine – where we again had to look more "wife material" rather than every man's fantasy, and even wear a wedding ring (it was the requirement for the mag). He took great photos and really made me feel comfortable. He also paid well and took me out to lunch after. He was so great I wanted to recommend him to others and I asked if he'd be interested in booking some of my girls off my books. He said yes and the majority of girls who worked for me ended up doing their first ever magazine shoot with him and all of them enjoyed it. Plus I made a finder's fee per girl.

Bold Behaviour

With my chlamydia cleared up and tests coming back negative, I decided to work more with Crystal. She'd asked me to go see her and do some more girl-girl shoots for a couple of amateurs. She had one of her regular guys pay us for two hours and would always manage to stagger the shooting time by allowing him to watch us wash in the bath and kiss and flirtatiously play with one another, a lick of a nipple, a boob squeeze, a stroke of a thigh. Then it was a case of drying off, choosing what to wear etc. By the time we did all that he only had about an hour of shooting to do, but her photographers never complained. With the pro photographers though, they shot per shoot so the quicker we acted the better. We did a shoot for a tog whose website was a custom one for wearing petticoats. Apparently, there was quite a fetish for it – I had never even contemplated that "slips" were sexy. But I'm guessing this may have been for the slightly older generation? Who knows. People paid memberships and as long as the photographer made money, I guess he couldn't care less who was signing up. And we certainly didn't care as long as we got paid.

After two weeks of being back from America, I finally showed my face to my staff and made out it wasn't a big thing that it didn't work out for me over there. Dee's husband, my uncle, had cancer and was not in a good way, so I took back the job of booking girls in for fresh shifts and just allowed her to let the girls confirm their shifts on the day of work.

I told Granddad that the Agent tried to get me to work with men in LA and that I'd told her to piss off and he said I'd done the right thing, and reiterated the "no man will ever want you if you do that" speech and I just replied back "Yes, I know, I *didn't* do it!" To a certain degree, my Granddad still scared me a bit with his deep loud voice. I remember as a child we would watch fictional cop shows on TV and if there was ever a storyline about someone on drugs Granddad would say:

"If I ever catch you doing drugs, I'll beat you into the middle of next week!"

I was only about eight at the time, but my goodness he drummed it into me. And other than alcohol, I'd never touched a drug. So the fear of Granddad (not God, but Granddad) was put upon me:

No drugs, no sex with men on camera. Noted.

(Just girls then – at least it wasn't all bad.)

22
TWINNING

A friend asked if I and one of my dancers would dress up sexy to podium dance at a club he DJ'd at up in Hertfordshire. They would pay for our travel, accommodation and drinks if we danced for free. Now usually I would say no, but my friend said there may be an opportunity there to put on a lap dance event; this, plus the option of a free night out in another county enticed me to say yes.

I took Lydia with me as she was always up for a night out away from her abusive boyfriend Shaun (it was a vicious circle; she drank more because he beat her, he beat her the more drunk and annoying she got). She had men queueing up to date her, more so because she had been put on the map by the Girl Channels and the newspaper, but like most people who are in abusive relationships, she'd been manipulated to believe she couldn't do any better than him. She came to me for pole lessons because he had had an affair and she wanted to feel better about herself. When he was found out, she didn't break up with him, I think maybe because her Dad had done the same to her Mum years ago and they had worked through it, so thought she could do the same. Lydia wasn't married to Shaun and had only been with him for a couple of years. But if you're going to work through an affair, you need to clean the slate and have no hatred. Lydia *did* work through the hatred, after pissing on his toothbrush every morning for a few months and putting laxatives in his tea so that he only just made it to work every day before needing the toilet. When she became a dancer the job never bothered Shaun; in fact I think he got off on her gyrating on other men. He had often told her he wanted threesomes, but she was completely against the idea. His reasoning for becoming violent never really came to light, but obviously she needed a breather every so often.

On the night, we each had a podium to dance on and after two songs Lydia joined me on mine, where we danced suggestively together to gain the attention of the people down on the dance floor. Afterward we joined the manager for drinks in the office and I managed to get a date booked in for a one-off event at their club on a Sunday – when they don't usually open. I said I'd come up each weekend to promote the night and to sell tickets. A free night out paid off well, although I had to put in a lot of the ground work.

There were a lot of hot men in this club; the grass is greener and all that. As I was walking round one Friday night there, a guy standing on his own said hi to me. I just smiled and walked off. I can be ridiculously socially inept at times, even doing the job I do, all the more when I'm not prepared. I had only just arrived so was getting my bearings and preparing myself to create the big sell with the tickets. Much later, I saw him again, with another guy. Who was cuter than him.

Jason was about six feet tall, smartly dressed in a shirt and jeans. We did the intros and I explained I wasn't from the area, and that I was at the club to sell tickets to a lap dance event I was running there in a few weeks. He bought a ticket and then began to talk to other guys about the event and either called me over to him to sell more or would send the men over to find me. Jason seemed to know a lot of people and the club was pretty big so I assumed he was a local who had been going there for years. Being quite flirtatious with me and helping out as best he could with the start of selling tickets, he deserved a kiss at the end of the night as he walked me to my car. I gave him my number and he suggested he and his friends should come to Kent one weekend.

Twinning

"Sure" I said, and thought nothing more of the passing comment.

Tuesday I received a text.

> "Hi Holly, it's Jason. It was nice meeting you last Friday. Can me and my friends come down this weekend?"

Something I wasn't expecting. I didn't know them, but I figured I could have a couple of my friends stay over to make me feel more comfortable about three complete strangers in the flat. I had such a big flat that the spare room upstairs could have housed eight double beds.

> "Yes that's fine, you'll have to come down after 7.30 though as I'll be working" (in one of the Friday afternoon bars I ran - a fantastic pub where we only danced on stage but it was a great earner – labourers would come in on their way home from work).

I wasn't going to turn that down just to be waiting at home for them.

> "Okay great, we'll see you then."

I was working with Alicia that day, and asked if she and her boyfriend wanted to stay down for the weekend – they would be my safety blanket. She fancied a break away from London so she agreed.

Jason, Steve and Aaron were waiting for me when we returned home. Once I'd shown everyone to their rooms to dump their stuff off, we congregated in the kitchen for drinks and all got ready to go out. I suggested that night we could walk to the pub in town, have a couple of drinks, and then they ran a return bus service from there to the nightclub a few towns along that only cost £5 each, much cheaper than a cab. It was a huge nightclub that held 2500 people (a larger capacity than the club I met them at in Hertfordshire) so I thought they'd enjoy going. They went along with it, as they knew nothing about the nightlife in Kent.

"Do you want one?" Jason said to me, holding out his hand when I was pouring a drink.

I looked down. It was an ecstasy tablet.

"No thanks, I don't do drugs." And continued to pour my drink.

Twinning

He looked a little awkward as I'd turned down his offer. Everyone else took one and I just let them get on with it. It now dawned on me as to how he knew so many people and why people would listen to him at the club in Hertfordshire when he was getting them to buy tickets from me. He was a dealer for pills. It's not the first time I'd hung out with people who did drugs, and usually ecstasy takers were happy and not paranoid. So I had hope that we were still going to have a great night out. And we did. We drank, we danced and we had a great time. It was good to have new friends and it was nice to have someone that liked me who wasn't from the area where I lived. Oftentimes when going out at weekends, I would bump into men that attended the venues I ran and had also seen me dance, and for whatever reason, whilst they were nice to my face, they repeatedly put me down to anyone who took an interest in me, or taunt them for wanting to date a stripper. The result? Men backing off from me *all* the time. But they couldn't get to Jason.

We got home around 3.30am – the bus ended up dropping us off outside of the town – apparently that was the norm as residents complained about High Street drop offs, but I didn't know as I rarely took the bus there and usually drove. We were all drunk so walking a mile at that time, even with us girls in heels, was pretty doable. Jason held my hand all the way home. And although we kissed, I didn't share a bed with him that night – I let him share a room with the others.

I woke in the morning before all of them and I needed to go and see my Granddad for a couple of hours. So I left them a note, with directions as to where things were in the town, along with a spare key and said I'd be back later. Once at Granddad's I took a nap on the sofa for a bit as I had struggled to sleep with so many people in the house. Jason texted me to tell me they were going out for lunch, so I went home knowing I could get some more sleep. Having lived alone for so long and being brought up as an only child meant I liked my space, so just a few hours helped me to press the reset button for some mental tranquillity before they all came back. And when they all came back, all five of them burst into my room and jumped on my bed with me on it. Then they left Jason alone with me to playfight.

He and I had a heart to heart and I explained how I hadn't had sex with a man since the year before when I'd caught chlamydia off my "friend" Greg, and we talked about how important sexual health is to both of us and how Jason had a near experience of catching something off a girl.

By the time we came out of the bedroom Alicia had made all the guys put face packs on before getting ready to go out. Jason had had a narrow escape by being in the room with me. I lived opposite a kebab shop and we could see directly into their shop from my living room window. Alicia and Aaron went into the shop to order food with green face packs on whilst we watched the shop owner do a double take as they came through the door and placed our food orders. We watched on from my first floor laughing at the mortified shop owner. It was great having fun with near strangers and I hadn't laughed so much in ages.

We did the same thing again that night; we went out to a club (a different one) and had a great night. Except when we got home, Jason spent the night in my bed and we had sex all night, and all morning. By late afternoon Sunday we said our goodbyes and I knew I would see him again as I would be in Hertfordshire to sell tickets for the event. He texted or called me every day and we planned for me to go up there the following week and stay with him for a couple of days.

Once I was back there, Jason began to tell me about his background; he was a twin and said his brother Kevin was the black sheep of the family; the money stealer, the liar, the guy who stole from their joint business venture and the one who caused family feuds. You name it, Jason said Kevin had done it. That was the main thing that he spoke about: Kevin. Kevin rarely went out though because he was in a relationship and had a child on the way, so I wouldn't be meeting him anytime soon at the club.

We went out that night to the club as it was open mid-week, and Jason's usual selling of pills went on, with the assistance of Steve; even in the week, when they were to go to work the next day, people still took drugs. I just got drunk, stayed away from the dealing and danced with Aaron; he and I had become dance partners since they came to Kent, and being the gay man that he was, he always styled it out. The end of the night came, Jason and I went back home and had more sex until he collapsed onto the bed saying:

"You'll be the death of me, Holly."

I took that as a compliment, because if he was going to die, what a way to go!

I left the next morning to make my way home and texted Jason to let him know I'd got back safely. I didn't hear anything that night from him. Or the next night, or the next. I rang Aaron to check everything was okay with Jason (just in case he'd been caught with drugs) and Aaron said yes, they'd been out on Friday night. It took until Saturday for Aaron to get Jason to call me to tell me he didn't want anything serious so didn't want to see me again. Our week to two weeks of fun was over and it shouldn't have bothered me, but it did. I was really upset as we'd had such a good time together when we were together. I guess I'd done the usual building up the fantasy of a new boyfriend in my head, when the reality of it was that I didn't know this guy; I'd only spent about four days with him in total. And the awkward bit was that I still had to go to the club to promote the event I was hosting. Aaron said Jason had only recently broken up from a pretty heated relationship so that's probably why he didn't want to be with anyone new.

I threw myself back into working weekends and took a couple of weekends off from going up to Hertfordshire. I wasn't earning much dancing, the venues didn't seem to be doing too well, so with a combination of that and Jason not wanting to see me anymore I began to feel unbalanced. I felt jittery, like everything was out of my control, and I used to wake up from crazy dreams, and one time having a panic attack which would start in my sleep. Then one afternoon I checked in to Auntie Dee's to update the diary and see how Uncle was and when I arrived the air was heavy.

"He passed away an hour ago." she said, holding back tears.

I, on the other hand, couldn't. I just sat there and cried after hugging Dee. I didn't know what else to do. My other Aunties and Uncles turned up to pay their respects, and my cousin Carla stayed out of the kitchen where we congregated, and she just flitted from room to room, cleaning and keeping busy – doing anything to prevent herself from accepting the reality of what happened. Fuck cancer. He looked so well around Christmas time when I'd seen him, and this was only a few months later.

I left as I told Dee I'd go and tell Granddad. I let myself in and he was sitting in his usual tub chair in the lounge. As I closed the door he said to me:

"Alright Babby?"

I looked at him and the tears welled up in my eyes again. His face dropped. And he shook his head:

"Oh no." He knew. "When?" So I told him. And we hugged whilst we both cried.

I cried a lot on and off; days, weeks later. I managed to work but struggled when I got home. Nothing felt right. My family were going through so much upset and Granddad struggled too. Nothing was in my control. And I still felt awful over Jason. I bought a fresh set of razor blades and started to cut my arms again. It's all I could do, it's the one thing I *could* control; a pain to inflict upon myself as and when *I* wanted to.

Twinning

I had to face facts. I needed to speak to Granddad. I wanted to talk to him like a child talks to their parent. I had to raise my voice so he could hear me. I held his hand, trying not to cry:

"I'm not well." He understood what I meant. "And I need to call someone"

"Okay," he said. "Are you going to get them to come visit you here?"

I nodded. I rang the mental health team and was seen as an urgent case referral so they came out within 24 hours and took some notes. They said they would be in touch with me to see a counsellor. I explained that no antidepressants work for me (I had tried several different types when Martin and I were going through our separation), so they couldn't suggest I go and see the doctor for a prescription. There was a little bit of a waiting list, so I decided to pay to see a psychiatrist.

I drove beyond the large iron gates of the clinic and followed the shingle driveway to the entrance of the building. My appointment was in a small room with two chairs, a desk and some bookshelves – no different from an NHS therapist's office. After giving a very nice man my life story from the start (omitting the rape as I didn't want to talk about it), the psychiatrist said:

248

"You have been shat on from a great height several times."

He diagnosed me with GAD – Generalised Anxiety Disorder

"...brought on by abandonment and rejection" from my parents.

"No pill in the world will cure what you're suffering from. All too often people get prescribed medication for their mental health yet it just numbs the problem and eventually one day it will blow up again. With or without medication, the best bet is to go to therapy and talk it through."

He wrote a report for me to take to my Doctor and give to whichever counsellor I was going to see. But my anxiety got worse before it got better. I started to shake when it got really bad and stutter on occasion when I spoke and I'd forget words. So I was prescribed beta blockers, which were mainly used for heart issues and high blood pressure. But if you have anxiety and tremors, they prevent adrenaline from working hard and making contact with the heart's receptors. And they worked for me. They slowed me down. They helped immensely whilst I waited for an appointment to discuss my life in depth.

Twinning

I found it easier to continue with my life in general. I went back to Hertfordshire to carry on promoting the big lap dance event. Aaron and Steve were out but Jason apparently had got back with his ex, so was having a night in. I recognised a few of the girls hanging around them but I didn't recognise the guy with them.

"Who's that?" I asked Aaron.

"Oh him? That's Kevin. Jason's brother…"

23
THE ROSES 'ROUND THE DOOR

Kevin didn't look much different from Jason. He had been welcomed into the peer group as he and his girlfriend had split up, despite the fact their baby was due in a couple of months, and he had moved in with Jason. I didn't say much to him as he appeared to be pretty quiet. But apparently, he knew who I was and that I'd dated Jason. He'd copped off with one of the younger girls in the group, Beth. "He didn't waste much time" I thought. I guessed he was just getting back on the horse quickly to make himself better like a lot of people do after a breakup. Aaron also liked him, but Kevin had given no indication to anyone that he was into men.

Within a couple of weeks Kevin was texting me. He'd obtained my number secretly from Jason's phone. He seemed fairly sweet, not laying any flirtation on particularly thick, but saying he was sorry for his brother's treatment of me and that Jason shouldn't have got back with his ex.

"That's nice of you to say so" I replied.

"Where do you live?" He asked.

"Kent."

"I'm bored, can I come down and see you?"

"When?"

"Tonight?"

"Don't you have work tomorrow?"

"I can leave early in the morning, it's fine."

And seeing as I was bored, I said yes and he made his way down to me.

We chatted over tea (it was the middle of the week, so we didn't drink) and he filled me in about his recent break up.

"It's hard living back with Jason. We don't get on all that well. Most people think that because we're twins we have an intense bond, but we don't. We used to own a company together and he stole all the money from it so we had to dissolve it…"

"Well according to Jason," I interrupted, "it was you who stole all the money."

He raised his voice a little.

"It was *him!* Ask our Dad, he'd tell you it was Jason…you've met him before, right?"

I nodded (as I had met his Dad when Jason needed to go round and drop something off to him) and chose to believe Kevin. For all he knew I could have asked for his Dad's number then and there. Why had Jason been looking for sympathy from me when I hadn't even met Kevin and he didn't want anything serious? My mind raced.

Kevin stayed over, in my bed, but other than a kiss nothing happened. We cuddled and he was a gentleman. He wanted me to be his girlfriend and I said yes, but we agreed we'd keep our relationship under wraps for a bit whilst we got to know each other and because he had only recently split from his girlfriend.

I went up to Hertfordshire that weekend and Beth came over to the group in the club to say hi. She looked a little excited and pulled me to one side and asked if I could give her some advice, as I was a little older.

> "I really like Kevin, and I think he likes me. I think I'm falling for him after he and I spent time together the other week."

I had to play it cool.

> "Have you heard much from him this week?" I pried, to see if he was playing me.

> "No, not at all, but I think he's been busy working."

> "Right," I said "well the best thing to do then would be to flat out ask him, surely?"

He needed to put the girl out of his misery and I wasn't going to be the one to tell her.

"I guess you're right, I'll do it later. Thanks! Wish me luck." She walked off.

"No, I won't wish you luck" I thought.

Kevin walked over to me with Aaron in tow and I told him what Beth had divulged.

"Shit," he said. "Why did she come to you of all people?"

I shrugged.

"I'll sort it, don't worry."

"I'm not worried," I uttered, "I'm more concerned she'll be upset because you're not into her."

He walked away, leaving me with Aaron.

"Oh my God." Aaron's eyes widened.

"What?" I asked, looking at him confused.

"I don't believe it. *You're* into Kevin aren't you!?"

Goodness knows what kind of face I was pulling when Kevin walked away for him to get the equation right.

I let out a deep sigh:

> "Look Aaron, I'm trusting you not to say anything. He came down a few days ago, we're together but we want to give it a chance before everyone tries to meddle." He looked really shocked. "*Please*, I'm begging you not to say anything, *we* want to tell people when *we're* ready."

> "Okay. No problem."

> "Thank you!" I said, relieved.

I stayed in the cheap hotel by the club in case Jason came home, and Kevin said he'd come by later, but had a few people going to his house for a bit. People who had been buying pills off him and Steve as he was left in charge by Jason to make the money when he wasn't going to the clubs. I didn't fancy going there, not even for a couple of hours. Beth would be there too and Kevin had to let her down gently first; after all, that was his mess.

But the mess turned into a shitstorm. Aaron did not take things as well as I'd thought, and not only told Beth about us, he told Jason the minute he got home. Jason got really angry. From what I was told, it took about three guys to break he and Kevin up from having a full-blown fight. What was the problem? Jason and I were never together and he didn't want to be with me, so why would it matter if I dated his brother? Aaron just sat back and watched the squabble out of spite because he had a crush on Kevin.

The morning came and Kevin hadn't shown up to my hotel as he'd spent so much time trying to calm down everyone who'd decided to get involved in the drama. He rang me at 10 to explain.

> "I'll pick you up in an hour. Me and Nate (Kevin's friend) are coming back with you for the weekend. Fuck this shit and all these idiots." It seemed a wise choice.

I hadn't heard from Aaron after he went back on his word, and Kevin said he had in his head that something was going to happen between them even though Kevin had told him a few times that he was only into women. He didn't get his way so he stuck the knife in to all and sundry that night. I thought it best not to contact him at all in case I said something I would later regret.

Kevin, Nate and I decided we were going to go clubbing, and to treat ourselves as we'd had a shitty start to the weekend, Kevin wanted me to book a limo. A lot of the clubs down here were connected to limo drivers, so whenever limo passengers arrived they would jump the queues outside straight away. I called up Hannah and invited her too and she said she'd meet us at the club after work and would come back in the limo and stay at mine after. Kevin bought us a bottle of champagne in the VIP area. His business was thriving so he wanted to spoil us. And it was nice to be spoilt. He and I were joined at the hip in the club. He was more doting than Jason, and I couldn't stop smiling with all the attention.

"This is ridiculously too soon," he said, "but I think I'm falling for you."

It felt like a fairy tale; only a few days in and this guy liked me. And he promised me the roses around the door with the white picket fence. Every woman's dream back then. And being in my 20s, I never questioned how quick someone could fall for someone. Sometimes naivety can be cute.

We fell back in our limo and all the way home Hannah was hanging out of the sunroof, topless, swaying her body and arms from side to side, facing the cars behind us, who obviously had a pleasant drive home with the scenery. I was actually surprised they didn't crash into the limo. She had no qualms about being topless in the open, even when she wasn't working, and we egged her on by cheering and laughing as we slouched around on the limo seats.

Kevin slept in my bed again. We had a bit of foreplay but didn't go all the way. He said he didn't want to treat me like Jason had done. So I figured that by the time I went back to his the following weekend, that would be *the* night to actually sleep with him. I couldn't go up to the club on the Wednesday as I had a modelling job with Alicia. As much as I wanted to stay with Kevin all the time, we knew we both had to work.

****

The job was a girl-girl wrestling custom-made video for a client. We didn't know what to expect, but took a mixture of clothes. I drove Alicia to the guy's address in Surrey. The house was huge but the carpet didn't look like it had seen a vacuum cleaner in a long time and was thick with dog hair from his golden retriever.

The guy made us a cup of tea each and explained he had clients who request certain videos. So he records them, edits them, and sends them off to only one client. He had a script for us whereby we had to remember certain words that the client wanted to hear us say and certain actions we had to do…it had to start off with us saying:

> "I know you're wanking over this, Michael; we can see you, Michael, you're a naughty boy/bad boy aren't you, Michael?…"

Custom-made videos always had the client's name so it was more personal and it was their way of knowing it was *just* for them. I mean, it could be sent to different Michaels but the probability of them liking the same thing would be narrow. This particular client had a fondness for boob slapping. So as we built up the dirty talk we were to grab and grope our own boobs and slap as we progressed into the movie.

The videographer went out of the room to get the camera.

> "You have *got* to be kidding me" said Alicia. "What kind of shit have you got me involved with now!?"

> "You know, he never said any of this was a requirement, I just thought it was going to be a bit of girl-girl and that's it. I'm sorry," I said, "but the best thing we can do is get this over ASAP and then get the hell out of here."

The first scene we were totally naked for Michael's film. No stripping at all. We studied the script, remembered the words and actions – there was no girl-girl involved here, which was a shame as it may have passed the time easier, although seeing as I had sensitive nipples it may have hurt with Alicia doing it rather than myself. Michael particularly liked tit-slapping from underneath rather than on top apparently (who would have known there was a preference!?). The dialogue was getting more and more ridiculous; we were looking straight into the camera, trying not to be too repetitive but it was hard not to be. Tit slapping wasn't something I was at all familiar with, so other than the script I had nothing relatable to say. Towards the end of the short film, the videographer raised his hand to indicate we had to slap our tits faster and say:

"Wank, wank for me; go on, wank it hard, wank, wank, wank..."

and words to that effect, imagining that would be the point that Michael would be ready to bring himself off to completion watching the special film. We were trying not to laugh as the quicker we repeated "wank," the more it began to sound like "quack" and my mind digressed to this Michael guy getting himself off to farmyard noises.

The cameraman let us have a breather and let our tits cool down from all the slapping. Mine were very pink, Alicia's not so much as she had darker skin than I.

"That was bloody awful." I said to Alicia.

"Yep, what's next? I can't wait to leave here though."

"Same."

The videographer called us and we stepped into the room next door, which was covered in green gym mats, similar to what my old school used to use during indoor P.E. Again, we were naked.

> "I want you two to wrestle each other, whilst doing a bit of girl-girl. So one will pin one down and you'll kiss or touch a body part, the other will then break free, and so on. The loser will be the girl who comes first."

This seemed like it would be more fun than the last movie. Alicia and I had worked together on the girl channels and had done a couple of amateur girl-girl shoots together before.

We began standing up. Alicia grabbed a hold of me and put her leg underneath mine so I fell backwards, then she pinned me to the floor and kissed me and I giggled.

> "CUT" The videographer said. "*No* laughing, this has to be serious."

We felt like we were being told off by a schoolteacher. Perhaps it was the olfactory memories of the gym mats.

"Start again." Up we stood.

Same move, but now we just concentrated hard so we wouldn't laugh. Alicia kissed my neck once we fell to the floor, I pulled my legs up around her waist and turned her over so I was on top. I went down on her. With her thighs tightening around my head, she spun me back over and sat on my face, so I was forced to lick her more. She moved forward so we were in a sixty niner and licking each other. The videographer circled around us as we continued, holding the camera above us, moving down to our same level and doing close ups as we performed the girl-girl manoeuvres. The way he was filming the shots reminded me of live concert footage that you'd often see on the Music Channels on TV. I spun Alicia over as she had me, removed myself from her face and turned around quickly to pin her wrists down with one hand, whilst I reached down with my other hand and placed my fingertips on her pussy, to strum her hard and fast. She was close to orgasm, but in the thick of it I wasn't concentrating on my other hand anymore and she freed herself and sat up. She kissed me hard again and pushed me down on the floor, so I fell on my side, then rolled me onto my stomach. She pinned my arms above my head and straddled my back. Leaning forward she breathed into my ear and began to kiss my neck. I forgot to struggle anymore. Still holding down my wrists she moved her body off me and put one of her shins on my back to keep me in place. Then she licked her fingers, shoved her other hand between my legs and inserted two of them into my pussy. I wriggled my hands free, but she moved her whole forearm onto my back (her shin no longer on me) and added her weight whist she continued to finger fuck me back and forth. The cameraman focussed close up on my face, pressed side-on into the mat, then moved away towards my ass and legs to see what Alicia was doing to me. I stopped fighting and began to speed up my breathing:

"Do you surrender?" Alicia asked.

I didn't want to admit it, so remained quiet other than panting with breath.

"Do. *You.* Surrender?!" she asked again with conviction as she moved her fingers in and out faster.

"Yes! I screamed, "Yes! Yessssssss."

I let go of the tension and came all over her frantic digits, whilst my ass and hips jolted upwards in spasm. Alicia got off me, stood up and lifted her arms up victoriously, just like a fighter in the ring and I laid there, exhausted as the camera panned away.

The videographer was more than happy with our performance. He paid us and we left the dog-hair-ridden place. I personally wouldn't work for him again, but he was interested in booking some girls from my agency, so I said I'd be in touch the following week.

I called Kevin on the way home and told him about my day.

> "Your day seems a lot more interesting than mine – I've been landscaping gardens all morning!"

He'd taken on Aaron and Steve to work for him as they were both without jobs and he wanted to help them out, even though neither of them had any experience. I said to him his day must feel like being at the club all the time as it was with the same people, and he laughed.

> "I miss you," he said.

> "I miss you too. Have a good night and I'll see you on Friday."

> "Can't wait. I love you. Bye."

I smiled as I hung up the phone.

24
THE BIG LET DOWN

I drove up before the rush hour on Friday as Kevin had taken a half day at work. Jason was on holiday so I was allowed to stay at the house. I was going to stay until Sunday night, after the lap dance event at the club. I took my bag up to Kevin's bedroom and he followed. We kissed and things got a little heated, so I dropped to my knees and sucked his cock whilst he laid back on the bed. He came before he got chance to do anything with me, so I just figured he was a bit over excited as it had been a while, and maybe after the club we would take things further. We had the whole weekend together after all; there was no rush. I put my top back on.

"What shall we do for dinner?" I asked, "Go out or grab something in the supermarket to cook?"

"Oh I've already eaten and I'm not hungry now," he said bluntly, doing up his jeans.

His behaviour was a little different from what I had been used to. Knowing I was arriving at 5pm he would know I hadn't eaten dinner and being the gentleman (I thought) he was last week, I'd assumed he would have thought about what we were going to be doing food wise, and not eaten so we couldn't eat together.

"Besides," he said, "we have to get ready to go out soon as we're meeting people in the pub before we go to the club."

He didn't even have bread in the house for toast. And I didn't want to moan as he was my new boyfriend. So I kept quiet and didn't eat.

Already disappointed, I got ready for the night ahead and Aaron turned up at the house very early; probably to try to prevent Kevin and I from doing anything together. He was unaware he had failed at that. Kevin went to a tin in a cupboard in his bedroom that had a bag of pills in and he picked out a handful to sell for the night. He had a baby on the way and I thought he was being an idiot dealing drugs, but I didn't say anything as it was his choice.

I stayed with Aaron in the pub whilst Steve and Kevin mingled, meeting people outside to exchange the narcotics for money. I stayed pleasant with Aaron, and pretended that what he did last week to stir the pot hadn't wound me up. After all, Kevin and I were out in the open now, so nothing could get in our way. At least that's what I thought.

When we arrived at the club, the atmosphere of the group was a little unsettled. Beth wasn't talking to me and wouldn't even look at me. She still look longingly at Kevin. There were a couple of new people hanging around the group – a tall blonde girl called Anna and her mum. Anna had told her mum to come out as she was fed up at home, and Kevin appeared welcoming and bought them a couple of drinks. He didn't offer to buy me one. Kevin hardly spoke to me and just hovered around the two of them.

"I've got something to tell you." Aaron said. "You see that girl Anna?"

"Yes," I thought, here we go again, more stirring…

"Well, Kevin met her in the club on Wednesday night and she gave him a blow job."

"*What*?" I said.

"I'm only telling you for your own good. The reason I didn't want you to be with him in the first place was because I knew he wasn't a good guy…"

"Don't lie!" I interrupted "Aaron, the reason you didn't want me to be with him was because you thought you could turn a straight man gay and wanted him to yourself."

I walked up to Kevin.

"Can I have the door key?" I asked. "I'm not feeling too good and I need to go back."

He could see I was upset about something, not showing any tears, but pissed off.

"Sure." He handed me his key. "I'll ring you when I'm on my way home so you can let me in."

I gave a false smile and said bye, and gave Anna a look as I walked on. I was shaking. The beta blockers didn't seem to be working. Worse, I had been drinking so couldn't drive home. I'd only had a couple of drinks but I didn't want to chance it. So there I was, in a strange house, with nothing to do but lie down and wait for Kevin to call.

He tried to call me several times about an hour later but I was too angry to pick up. Then Aaron called.

"Are you okay?" He asked.

"What do you think?!"

"Kevin thinks you're going to steal all his pills."

I laughed:

"I don't even touch that shit, why would I be interested in stealing them? He's an idiot." I hung up.

Kevin stopped calling so Aaron must have told him what I said. Either that or lied about it.

They turned up after 2am. I let them in. They left the door ajar as more people were due back. Kevin had no respect for the fact that I was pissed off with him and had still invited people home for an after party.

"What's up with you?" He asked.

"Are you *kidding* me!? You're *actually* asking me a dumb question like that?!" I said angrily. I felt like my eyes were going to pop out of my head.

He grabbed my wrist really hard and dragged me upstairs. I told him he was hurting me and he loosened his grip a little. Then when we were in the bedroom, the first thing he did was go to the pill tin. I laughed.

"Like I told Aaron on the phone, I couldn't give a toss about your pills, I don't even touch them, *why* would I want to take them?"

He looked at me.

"I'm not the one being dishonest here Kevin, am I? Seriously, I couldn't get up here on Wednesday and you can't wait so get your cock sucked by someone else! *After* you tell me on the phone that you love me! You're disgusting."

"I didn't do that."

"Save your bullshit, Aaron couldn't wait to tell me, just like he always can't wait to tell anyone about whatever you're up to."

He went to go and find Aaron, and Beth was on the landing near our bedroom. She was probably trying to listen in on our conversation.

"And *you* (I pointed at her), you stupid little girl, need to stop following Kevin around like a little lost sheep because he has absolutely no interest in you and doesn't even like you! *Get* away from me." She skulked off and knew not to come near me again.

It's amazing how quickly someone can pull the wool over your eyes. Clouded judgement does no favours. He even had the audacity to invite Anna back that night with everyone else, but either he or Aaron had messaged her to explain it wouldn't be a good idea. I was seeing red and I didn't just blame Kevin. It takes two to tango. I went to bed, not that I managed to sleep as I was livid, on top of the party with the pill heads downstairs. Kevin slept in Jason's room. The morning came and I told him I was going to drive home and just drive back up Sunday night for the event.

He took me to lunch, by way of a lame-arsed apology and to try to restore some sort of civility between us. He and his friends were coming to the event on the Sunday and quite frankly I didn't want them *not* coming, as it was more potential money for the girls - it was important I kept my personal issues separate from my business. But he didn't take me to lunch on his own. Aaron wouldn't leave his side and *had* to come along. He was like a wart you couldn't remove. And he remained determined to have Kevin one way or another.

I was still in a bit of a daze that everything had taken a 180° as quickly as it did. I rang my older friend Ron for a catch up as I'd seen him the week before at the club and introduced him to Kevin and Nate. I explained what Kevin had done:

> "Well girl, you've only just met him, you shouldn't have been jumping in so quick to trust him."

> "I know, Ron, but he must have liked me because he drove all the way down to see me that one time and then the following weekend"-

> "Can I give you some advice from a man's perspective?" he asked.

> "*Please* do!" I replied.

"I'm going to be blunt. Pussy's pussy. Near or far, men don't care, and if it's on the table and we want it, we'll find a way to get it…"

25
GENTLEMEN'S EVENINGS

As the warmer weather approached, I would get more requests to book strippers for stag and hen nights and sometimes milestone birthdays. Usually one male or female stripper would turn up at the house or pub where the celebrations were happening, already in his/her attire (usually a uniform like a nurse's outfit/ police/ sailor). They would be shown who the Stag/Hen was, sit them down on a chair and then perform in front of them with a lap dance and something "extra" whilst they stripped (for instance, putting baby oil on their hands and getting them to rub it in on them). Everyone else in the party would cheer them on. The stripper would get paid a set amount and I got about £10 or £20 per job as commission.

Gentlemen's Evenings

Then there were gentlemen's evenings. Rugby clubs, working men's clubs and football clubs especially used to book them. The venue would sell tickets to guarantee an audience and make sure they could pay the dancers and a comedian (who would generally compere the evening) to secure the night. When dancers worked gentlemen's evenings (which we called "stag dos" most of the time), they got a fixed fee to perform two shows. In addition, if two girls were booked they'd usually do a jug collection at the end and split the money between them and do a double act (it was up to the girls how heavy they wanted to go), but they would usually tell the guys the more they put in the better the show would be.

Now there were two types of "stag" girls; normal and "blue." Blue girls did heavier shows; either with insertion of toys or during the two girl act, performing a sex act of some sort on a guy from the audience. This is another reason I think tickets were bought in advance: so venues could have the event as private, with closed doors and only those with tickets could attend. Sometimes I'd get asked to book girls in for gents' nights and I'd have to ask the type of girl they wanted, so as not to disappoint the clientele. These weren't always in Kent; girls who did stag nights would drive all over the country. A bit like the roadshows, although with roadshows we were never paid a basic.

One day a friend of mine called up to ask if I could take her place on a local stag show with a compere and another girl. A blue girl.

This particular night was at a rugby club. I, being the "clean" girl, was the "warm up" and the blue girl would do her own show later. I said as long as whoever booked it only expected me to do a clean show, I'd do it.

I arrived at the rugby club and the changing room was available for the comedian and the two of us girls. There was a door leading out onto a small, carpeted stage in the hall, where the men gathered at the bar or sat at tables. The comedian set up his sound system and began telling jokes, prepping the guys and getting them even rowdier for me, the first girl on stage.

> "Are you ready?!" he yelled over the microphone, which reminded me of the set-up of the Essex club on my first shift, with me waiting nervously in the wings.
>
> "Reeeeeeeh!" they shouted back like Neanderthals.
>
> "Please give a warm welcome tooooooooo… Holly!!!"

The comedian pressed play for my songs. I came out in a school girl uniform and the men cheered. I stepped off the stage and danced from table to table as there were a lot of guys and the stage wasn't particularly high for them to all see. I also thought some audience interaction may help gain their praise. I removed my tie and put it around the back of one guy's neck and with it, pulled his head into my cleavage. He smiled and played along, shaking his head in between whilst his friends cheered. Moving to the next table I made another guy unbutton my shirt. The guys loved this, as in the usual strip clubs and pubs there was no touching allowed. This is what separated the private, ticketed events from public ones, and probably why men were more keen to attend.

I grabbed another man and pulled him up on stage. I pulled his jeans down to just under his bum cheeks, bent him over a chair, and keeping in with the college theme I picked up my prop…a cane. I stood to the side of him, so the audience could watch and I caned him. Every time he bolted upright when the cane touched him, and every time I bent him back over. Everyone laughed at him and yelled at me to continue. I caned him four or five times, enough to build up the crowd but prevent the "victim" getting too annoyed. He was a good sport. My first show had gone down well.

The comedian continued to entertain the crowd and I went backstage with my clothes. The blue girl, Avril, had shown up during my spot as she had travelled a little further than me. Whereas my prop was a cane, Avril's was a banana. I don't need to explain where she was going to stick it. I wondered how the men would still like my next show after hers. Surely it would seem a little more mundane? But I'd been paid my basic so I carried on in my cowgirl outfit, picking out a guy in the crowd with a belt and removing it from him. I made him get on all fours and sat on his back. With the belt loosely round his neck I made him out to be my horse and tapped his butt with my hand saying "Giddy up" whilst he paraded around with me on his back. Everyone was laughing, including me, making sure he wasn't going so fast that I would fall off. They didn't seem phased that I wasn't inserting fruit into myself like the other girl and I still got a round of applause.

After Avril's next show, she and I were to do a girl-girl performance but I gave her notice and told her outright I only imitate girl-on-girl acts. I didn't know her, and didn't want her licking me or me going near her as I had no idea where she'd been. I didn't want a scare, especially after what happened during my drunken Christmas ordeal with Greg; and yes, you can catch chlamydia going down on a girl or a guy. Avril didn't do films so didn't get regular checks like I did. And thank goodness I said what I did before she went out for her next blue show…

…I had never seen a blue show, so I decided once she was out there performing, to open the door slightly so I could peep out. She pulled a man up onto the staging and got him to lay down. She unzipped his jeans whilst the music played on, and sat on his cock. Not a condom in sight. He laid there motionless. From what I managed to see, he didn't stay hard so she soon got off him. But the thing that stuck out the most during this show – and it obviously wasn't this gentleman's penis – was that where the guys had been egging me on, cheering and laughing, they were completely silent with her performance. Perhaps it was all too much? I know that when Avril and I went to do the jug collection for our double act, some audience members said:

> "You've done a much better show than her and you didn't even need to do what she did."

I was glad they accepted me for what I did and were still happy to put money in the pot.

The two-girl show we delivered was pretty poor. Pretending to do something to someone can be done in such a way that guys can still *think* you are doing it (I learned that during my webcamming time). But Avril did everything too over the top and too fast, so they could tell she was totally faking it. She made it hard for me to work with her. I just hoped the song would be over soon. By this time the guys were fed up. I think they'd seen too much pussy (and quite possibly, fruit) and just wanted to drink their beer. Nevertheless our jug was pretty full and she and I split the collection. She got changed and shot off before I had even managed to put my money in my purse. I think she had a driver waiting for her. And she only ended up with £20 basic more than me for doing all the extreme things.

The comedian was talking to me as I got changed. It didn't faze me; I was used to sharing rooms with male strippers or comedians, no different to theatre shows either, I guess – you can't be shy in these sorts of situations. He went off to load his car up with his sound gear whilst I continued to pack my outfits away. Everything was all zipped up and he came back to say goodbye.

> "Thanks for the job," I said to him "let me know if you need me for any other jobs down this way" and gave him my number.

> "No sweat." He said, and went to give me a hug.

I hugged him back and went to give him a goodbye kiss on the cheek. But as I tried to pull away he moved his head, still holding me in more of an embrace, than a hug, and tried to tongue my mouth. I pulled away and just laughed it off and said:

> "Come on, don't be silly, I need to go now."

He looked a little confused that I'd refused him and I just got my bag and wheeled it out, still smiling as I said:

> "Bye!"

I didn't want him to make anything up to other comedians so they wouldn't book me for future work and he may well have done that if I had hurt his ego by being stern. But that was the first and last time I was to ever see him. Thankfully.

26
" PROOST "

I scoured *The Stage* newspaper once more, along with a website for strippers to find more work for the dancers on my books. I found an agency, based in Amsterdam, looking for webcam models and dancers for contracts throughout Europe. I dropped them an email to see if they would be interested in working with me and we would then share the commission. They said they might be and suggested I fly over for a meeting. Back then, flights were dirt cheap. I'm talking less than £50 for a day return to most countries in Europe.

Abel and Isaak met me at the airport and we got a train into the main part of the city. I was wearing a suit to be professional, but the two of them arrived looking like tourists – wearing ill-fitting jeans and scruffy pullovers. They took me around a webcam house, which was always in need of girls and couples (it would be a 14-day contract and whoever worked there, lived there too). They had separate private chat rooms, with beds or desks and chairs, dependent on the theme of the room, plus there was a camera in the kitchen/diner area, with a pole on the other side of the kitchen. The house was clean and seemed okay. They also took me to the outside of a club they wanted dancers for, although I couldn't go in as it only opened in the evening. Their other clubs were in other countries. We sat down in a little café opposite the club so I could take notes. I explained to Abel and Isaak that I would need to know the ins and outs of each club, club rules – if there's touching (I knew some clubs outside of England allowed it and I wanted to be honest with girls about expectations to avoid misunderstandings), house fees/commission, duration of contracts, if flights and/or accommodation were included and so on. They realised how thorough I was and I stated that I wouldn't send a girl to somewhere where they wouldn't feel comfortable or obligated to stay somewhere they wouldn't like, as that would cause more trouble for us and we wouldn't get our commission. I told the story about the two girls I knew who'd visited Greece two years before and the club there trying to take their passports away. As a dancer myself, I refused to put a girl's life in jeopardy.

I went through all the clubs' details with a fine-tooth comb. Abel remembered most of the itinerary of each club by heart. Along with the Amsterdam venues, I was offered clubs in Luxembourg, Germany, Portugal and Belgium (there were three in Belgium). All were champagne clubs – make commission on selling champagne first, then get the dances as an extra top up. As before, when I looked into European clubs, accommodation was cheap, there was transport to the club if necessary, flights were reimbursed if girls stayed for a minimum of two weeks, the fees were all 50-50 and commission on drinks depended on the size of the bottle of alcohol. But unlike the club in Ireland I danced in, the drinks were fully alcoholic and it was encouraged to sell bottles of champagne if possible, rather than by the glass.

Upon my return home, I let my girls know the ins and outs of these new opportunities.

I decided to try working in the club in Amsterdam for myself for a week. The boss of the club wanted me to train some of their dancers in the afternoons for a few days, like I did with my Academy in England, and the girls would pay me each day. I flew over during the UEFA Euro matches, so Amsterdam was pretty busy in all the bars. I stayed in a little hotel next door but one to the club. It was a champagne club, and you could sell dances but it was 50 Euros for two dances; the customers couldn't pay for just one dance, which I thought very strange.

I started dancing on the Monday and training on the Tuesday. I walked into the dressing room and tried to say hello to the girls but they just looked at me vacantly, and continued talking in Dutch. I got changed and went downstairs.

The club was small. There was a catwalk-type stage with one pole that went right up into the dressing room. If you wanted to start your show from the dressing room and slide down onto the stage, you had to press a button to notify the DJ you were ready. I'd never seen a club that had that before. Dances were through a curtain at the back of the stage and there was only room for one girl and customer at a time. It made sense in a club like this, that selling champagne was more important.

After speaking to the boss, Richard, and finding out who I was, a couple of the girls introduced themselves to me and let me know I was teaching them the following day. We spoke for a little while, but then they went off and did their own thing.

I sat at the bar by the door. It was about 9pm when the first customer arrived. He sat right next to me; apparently I'd picked a good spot. I said hello. He was American. Turns out the club had a lot of

Americans come in as they fly over on business. Americans love an English accent, so this was a winning situation for me.

He ordered a beer and bought me a glass of champagne. I could feel the other dancers' eyes making daggers at me. My first night, and I bagged the first customer, *and* he didn't hesitate to buy me champagne. We sat and talked, I asked if he wanted a dance and he didn't, so we just continued to drink.

I wasn't one for drinking much champagne at the time, so I asked to have some water next to me on the bar, to which the barmaid obliged. I sipped that in between too, to try and dilute the bubbly.

Richard smiled at me from the end of the bar, pleased I was fitting in well. After three glasses of champagne, my customer said his goodbyes as he had to get a flight back the next day and I remained seated by the door. As he left, another guy came in. He sat next to me. Also American. I decided this could be a good seat for me for the duration of the evening. Again, he liked my accent, again he was over on business. This time, he bought a bottle of champagne for us to share. As we talked the same talk as before, I knew I had to get rid of some of the bubbly drink from my glass without him seeing. I excused myself and went to the bathroom, taking my drink with me. I poured all but a quarter of it away into the sink and then returned to my seat, where he gave me a refill.

" PROOST "

Wine or champagne gets me drunk far quicker than spirits. That's probably why I wasn't a fan. The lady behind the bar could see I was struggling so she came over:

> "Would you like a cube of ice in your drink so it's colder? (trying to dilute it as best she could for me)."

But my customer looked at her a little strangely, as our champagne was cold enough because the bottle was in a bucket. I politely but begrudgingly declined her offer to help.

There were a couple of potted plants in the corners near to the lower seats by the stage, but I was nowhere near to dispose of any of the alcohol in them. I had to ride this out. At one point he went to the bathroom so I asked the lady behind the bar to quickly pour away a whole glass and refill it again. I know I could have taken my time drinking but the trick was to drink as fast as possible in the hope that the customer would buy more champagne to share. And when he returned, he poured himself another glass but there was only enough to fill half.

> "Can we have another bottle please?"

> "Dancing is so much easier than this!" I thought to myself. "And less calorie consuming."

The customer stayed for another 45 minutes, without finishing the bottle.

"You can have the rest to yourself" he said, smiling at me before he left, as if he was doing me a favour.

The minute he was gone, I gave my glass and the rest of the bottle to the barmaid to pour away. I chugged on more water to try to keep a level head. A couple more customers came in but I think they were regulars and went directly over to the dancers they would usually visit. I was glad for the break as I didn't want to end up being sick.

It was an hour before anyone else came in and he sat down in a chair next to the stage to watch the shows. I moved out of my seat by the door and walked over to him and introduced myself.

"Please, sit" he said to me.

He was Dutch, but he had dark hair and dark eyes, different from the stereotypical blonde Dutch people I had seen. He called over the waitress and asked for a bottle of champagne. She carried over a bottle in a bucket full of ice in a stand and poured the first two drinks for us. We clinked our glasses together.

"Cheers" I said

" PROOST "

"Proost"

Because of where the guy was seated, it was easy to find things to talk about. Being next to the stage gave us the prompt to discuss stage shows and the music choices of the DJ and dancers. When he wasn't looking, I tipped some champagne into the plant pot next to us.

Time raced on and it was approaching 2am. We were now onto our third bottle. Sometimes I would put my glass down low and pour champagne onto the carpet. The soil in the plant pot was so moist I'm surprised the plant hadn't drooped through intoxication. The carpet was sodden. I had already visited the bathroom twice since sitting with him and poured some into the sink. I was running out of options and was glad it was nearly closing time.

I excused myself again and walked over to the waitress to ask her what time the club was to close:

> "We stop letting people in at 2, but anyone here still buying champagne can stay. Sometimes they don't leave until 7am."

> "7AM?! 7.A.M?!" I thought.

There was *no* possible way I could survive that long. I was feeling drunk and finding it hard to walk in a straight line as it was. I held onto her desperately and said:

"You *have* to help me! I can't stay and drink *an-y-more!*"

She just looked at me stunned. The owner was still sitting at the bar, so I walked back to my customer, poured some more champagne into my glass and then smiled whilst I placed my hand on his knee:

"Darling I won't be a second, the owner wants to speak to me, seeing as it's my first night here."

"Sure, no problem. Do what you got to do."

"Hi Richard, I have a bit of a problem" I said as I plonked myself down on the bar stool next to him.

"You do? What's that?"

"I'm not used to drinking as this is the first champagne club I've worked and I truly think if I stay any longer and drink anymore, I will actually throw up."

His shoulders moved a little as he chuckled:

"I thought you were going to tell me something serious."

"Well, I *am* being serious. I know that guy has money and is spending but I'm running out of ways to get rid of the champagne. I've visited the ladies' room twice to pour some away already." I waved at the barmaid. "Can I have a clean glass please?" She handed it over and I poured half of my glass into it so I had only a couple of centimetres left for when I returned.

"Have you tried pouring it into the plant pot next to you?" Richard asked.

"It's already full." I said

"Carpet?"

"Soaking wet."

Richard laughed again.

"You know, after 2am you are allowed to leave anyways but obviously it's in the club's and your best interests to stay as long as you like if you are still selling the bottles. But you

294

know what Holly? You've outsold everyone here for a Monday night, I've not seen anything like it in a while."

"*Really*!?" I said, impressed with myself. "Well look, I'll stay until the guy finishes this bottle if he wants me to then I'll go."

"No worries, I'll have your money ready."

I sauntered back over to my customer.

"Everything okay?" he asked

"All good," I replied. "He seems happy with me. Once we finish this bottle I'm probably going to call it a night as the champagne has gone to my head a little and I have training here with the girls tomorrow."

"Okay, what time does it close here tonight?"

"Until people stop buying champagne."

"I'll probably stay a little longer and maybe sit with another girl for a while."

I thought, well at least the club will still make money with him even when I've left.

"Has anyone else caught your eye?" I asked, thinking I could be polite and help him out as a goodbye gesture to him.

He looked around the perimeter of the club as best he could from where we were seated.

As it was past 2am some girls had already left, but there was a girl at the bar, with long blonde hair, with a customer who looked like he was finishing up his drink.

"What about her?" he suggested, pointing her out. "Do you know her?"

"I've not really spoken much to anyone tonight but she arrived when I was with a customer so never got to say hello."

"If her customer leaves, then yes, I'd like to talk to her."

We poured a little more into our glasses, and as we spoke, we both kept our eye on her and her customer. As we saw him stand up, I said to my customer:

"Okay, let me go get her."

"Thank you."

I hovered around until her customer walked away and then approached her.

"Hi." I smiled

"Oh my God you're English." She said, with an English accent.

"Yes, *I am!* As are *you*!" I said surprised, but also relieved there was someone here I could finally talk to. "I'm Holly" I held out my hand for her to shake.

"Jennifer, nice to meet you."

"Jennifer, I've drunk *way* too much and I'm not used to all this drinking, I'm more used to lap dancing…"

"It takes some getting used to!"

"Don't I know it! My customer is still going to stay when I've finished the bottle with him" I pointed over to him and

Jennifer and I waved coyly, smiling, "and he said he would like to have you sit with him so if you're not looking to leave yet do you want to come and join us and then continue with him when I've left?"

"My God, that is *so* nice of you! I've been here a year and no one has ever done that for me before!"

"Really!?"

"Yep, really, the Dutch girls tend to stick to each other like glue." She rolled her eyes.

"Well tonight, the English are sticking together," I said to her, "come with me."

I introduced her to him and we asked for an extra glass to give Jennifer some of the champagne.

"Oh my gosh – two English ladies in one night!" his eyes lit up.

We played on the fact we were both English and giggled and flirted. It was easier with a "wing woman." And bringing someone new into the dynamic meant we could ask her questions and drag the night out a little longer.

Jennifer lived in Amsterdam. She was originally from the north of England, and moved to Amsterdam when her mother relocated there. She had a daughter, but only told me that when the customer went to use the restroom:

"Mum has her when I'm working." She told me.

Realising we had run out of champagne, that was my moment to say my goodbyes to them both. That way, Jennifer would get the commission on the next bottle.

"Lovely to meet you." I kissed the customer on the cheek in the Dutch way (three kisses), and said to Jennifer "Are you in tomorrow?"

"Thursday"

"Great, see you then."

I picked up my pay packet.

" PROOST "

> "Good work" said Richard, "Especially making sure the customer will stay after you leave too."

> "Hey, that way I don't feel guilty about leaving!" I smiled and walked upstairs to go get changed.

I staggered back to my hotel room feeling very thankful that it was only two doors away. I chugged some water and fell into bed into a champagne-induced slumber.

Where some can sleep for longer after drinking alcohol, I cannot. My liver clearly likes to inform me that it's breaking down the booze to get it out of my bloodstream. I feel like I'm cooking from the inside. And my stomach also likes to punish me and speed up digestion – more so with champagne. So with lack of sleep and feeling lethargic, my stomach turning inside out and a craving for any fried carb-based foods, I knew this was going to remain a short trip. There was no way in this world, no matter how much money I made, that I could live this lifestyle without piling on the pounds and damaging my insides. I had no idea how the girls did this day in, day out and still looked slim and awake.

I managed to pull myself together by the late afternoon for teaching, but the girls weren't really interested. They could understand me perfectly as English was their second language, but most of the time just chatted amongst themselves in Dutch whilst I was trying to teach them "dancer etiquette," how to lap dance and how to own the stage. Over two days, the girls dropped out and not one paid me for their classes as Abel had promised me they would. Perhaps they didn't actually cope well with hangovers either, or perhaps they just thought they knew it all. As they began to drop out they stopped showing up for work too. More than likely because they thought I would chase them for their money. But what was the point, chasing them for something they didn't have? They weren't even selling champagne. You would think they would want to listen to me, especially as they were well aware I was selling far better.

Not teaching meant I could focus more on afternoon naps before work and explore around Amsterdam Square, including the coffee shops. I wanted to buy some weed as it was legal out there and I asked the guy behind the counter to roll one for me as I was incapable of even rolling a cigarette. No matter how much I try, I tend to fold rather than roll. I took the fresh spliff back to my room and smoked it. I felt no different and went to work a couple of hours later.

The following day I went back to the shop and said it had done nothing for me; did he have anything a bit stronger he could suggest for me off the menu? He rolled me another one and after a late breakfast in the Irish bar (inclusive of carbs to soak up the alcohol), I walked back to my hotel to spark up again.

I smoked half of it, giggled a lot to myself and passed out on my bed. I fell asleep for an hour and a half. When I awoke, I had pain in the middle of my chest and couldn't take much of a deep breath. I stood up and thought a walk might help, so I put my shoes on and went out, also thinking I'd grab a late lunch/early dinner. It was the weed giving me the munchies. I ate a *lot*, including ice cream. Still the pain wouldn't shift, but I lethargically got ready for work.

This was the first night I struggled. Everyone could see it. The chest pain did not ease. It was like a heavy feeling in the middle of my rib cage. The DJ offered me an indigestion remedy, which I took, although to me it didn't feel like indigestion. And I was right – the discomfort remained. I painstakingly attempted to sit with customers to click with them and get some champagne ordered but they looked disinterested. Perhaps I looked a mess, perhaps I looked in pain and they felt uncomfortable? I didn't know why I couldn't click; all I knew was this was the only night so far where I didn't make a penny. And it felt like a total write-off, as the more I sat alone, the more I realised I had nothing to distract me from the crushing feeling in my chest. I had to explain to Richard as he noticed how, for the first night, I didn't bring my A game. He laughed as he could see I clearly wasn't used to smoking weed or I wouldn't be suffering.

"Because you said the first stuff did nothing for you, he must have hit you with the hard stuff when you asked for something stronger!" He threw his head back and laughed out loudly.

"Well I'm glad you find it funny!" I said, sarcastically laughing at him.

"Look, you've been here a few hours and I can clearly see the pain hasn't dulled down at all, so why don't you go back to your hotel, sleep it off and come back in tomorrow night fresh? It's not as if I don't know you're a hard worker. Today was just a case of bad luck, which I know you won't do again."

So off I went back to my hotel room.

Once I reached my door I could smell the weed before I even opened it. The remaining weed was still in the bag I'd bought it in, in my jeans pocket. It stank out my whole room. I opened the windows to air out the room, rolled up my jeans and put them in two plastic bags, one inside the other, back in my suitcase to avoid having to smell the memory of why I had the chest pain. I certainly had no intention of smoking the rest after the earlier day's mistake. I fell asleep pretty easily and the next day I woke up with no pain. It *had* to have been the weed that caused it.

By the time Saturday night arrived, England were playing in the Euro Championships. The tables in all the bars of Amsterdam Square were full. When England scored a goal, the sound of cheering travelled all around the Square. The city was clearly full of English and right now, Amsterdam was a happy place to be.

Like the weekends in London, there was a different clientele in the strip clubs from during the week. No customers away on business utilising their time with a pretty lady over a bottle of champagne. Instead, there were drunken men on a weekend jaunt, either to watch the football, celebrate a stag night or just to go out and yell like juveniles.

Much to the pleasure and amazement of about six English guys in the club, they came across me and although a little inebriated and complaining about the price of beers, they stayed for a while, and each of them in turn bought me champagne by the glass. None were drinking any themselves, so they didn't want to buy a bottle. The Dutch girls that night seemed to deal with the Dutch men, I dealt with the English, and Jennifer dealt with both. I called her over one time and she managed to get a dance and a glass of champagne with one of the guys in my group. The others had dances with me individually (my last day at work in the club and the first time I'd done any dances) and because the club wasn't too busy and I couldn't see any other men not being "tended to," I thought it best to stay where I was. Gradual, steady money is better than no money, plus they were pretty polite and friendly.

It wasn't my best night of earning, but it certainly beat the day before. As I collected my last lot of pay from Richard, he said:

> "Do you think you can come back anytime soon? You earned us quite a lot of commission."

> "I would like to come back, but I'm not sure when yet as I have some contracts to deal with back home."

Plus I needed some time without alcohol! The club was a great earner for me but it just wasn't practical to go there too often. Getting drunk every night wasn't on my to-do list, and also I needed to be home for Granddad's hospital appointments. I had arranged for Dee to take him this week, but I know it was easier for me to be there the majority of the time so I could listen to what the specialists said.

" PROOST "

As I handed the key back to my room the next day, I walked past the club; the outside appeared so much tinier than it was inside. I knew it would be a nice little venue for the girls on my agency books, and I could now add this to the list of tried and tested clubs for them to work in.

I flew home, satisfied the trip had been worthwhile and my purse was full of money that I could exchange back into Sterling.

I also flew home with marijuana in my suitcase, within two plastic bags, within a pair of jeans, that I had totally forgotten about because the plastic bags had done the job of hiding the smell in my room that Friday night.

27
A CONFLICT OF INTEREST

Upon my return, Kevin was in touch with me again to ask if the group could come down one weekend from Hertfordshire for a night out and he'd hire another limo. All the boys in the group were now working for him and going out with him every weekend, allowing him to buy all the drinks, even though they now had their own money to spend.

I guess I'm a glutton for punishment, and even though he hurt me I still wanted to see him, so I said yes. I warned him that he should be careful about being too charitable towards all these people because one day, if ever his money ran out, I could bet my bottom dollar the so called "friends" he had wouldn't stick around.

A Conflict Of Interest

It was the usual fun evening, glasses full to the brim with champagne and dancing in the club. Amongst the group was Aaron. It wasn't enough that Kevin and I were no longer together. He still felt the constant need to chaperone us even after all the shit he'd thrown at us before.

Upon coming back to my house after the club, Kevin shared my bed, much to Aaron's dismay, who wanted him to stay in the same room as he and Nate. A couple of hours later, I heard my door slam and assumed one of the boys had gone out for a cigarette. But it was Aaron; he'd arranged for someone to pick him up, from an hour and a half away, because he was annoyed he didn't manage to share a bed with Kevin.

I had had enough of Aaron's childish mood swings and I couldn't be bothered to even call or text him to ask if he was okay because, quite frankly, it was blatant that he wasn't. Perhaps we could hold each other and cry whilst we competed verbally over who liked Kevin the most? Absolutely not. I had no interest in going back there after I knew this was to be their final visit down. For me, I guess you could call it closure. It was a great evening, but I was done. Done with Kevin being a super flirt and trying to bang anything he could, done with watching him be used by anyone who wanted money, and done with the general drama from his male friend who followed him around like a love-sick puppy, when Kevin told him time and time

308

again he was straight and not interested in him or any other guy. They could all be someone else's problem. As a goodbye gift (although Kevin didn't realise this was the last time I intended on seeing him), I gave him the marijuana I'd accidentally "smuggled" back from Amsterdam as I for sure didn't want it.

That night he called me.

> "I've just smoked that stuff you gave me...I've got a massive headache!" I could hear him panting.

I giggled:

> "I gave it to you as I thought it was only too strong for me because I'm not used to it."

> "I'm too hot, I need to take my top off. I can't believe how strong this stuff is!"

I must have bought the strongest weed in the coffee shop. When I texted Kevin the next day, unlike me he didn't have the chest pains as I'd had.

I didn't hear from him much more after that weekend, except for the time work dried up, leaving him with no income.

"You were right," he said, sounding deflated, "none of them want to hang around with me now I can't pay for their drinks."

There was no point telling him I told you so, because I knew he would still strive to win their friendship again somehow. He was no longer my problem and Hertfordshire and everyone in it was out of sight, out of mind. I had dance contracts to focus on, a new one over here and several venues abroad to send girls to.

My new contract over here was arguably a conflict of interest. It was a five-minute walk from the Cellar bar venue that I had been putting girls in for over a year. The landlord now had my girls there on a Sunday and Thursday, and a blue show every so often (provided by another agency). I told the owner, Todd, I had been asked to go look at the venue opposite and that I would report back to him and see what they wanted.

It turns out the manager of the pub opposite had been to the Cellar bar to check it out. They wanted to run things slightly differently. They had a pole they were going to install upstairs, to try to entice customers to come downstairs for dances. But the only place they could put the pole was on a podium with a 45 degree slant to it. Immediately I could see this was a dumb idea. They wanted to run it on a Tuesday and have topless dances only downstairs and no jug collection, somewhat different from the nude dancing Cellar bar. The manager, sounding very ambitious, said:

"When things really pick up here, we'll have it every night."

I explained not to walk before he could run and that people in a small town only have so much money to spend on dancers. It's not as though we're London with a constant passing trade. He wanted to start in two weeks' time so I said I'd get back to him.

Upon leaving, I went straight to the Cellar bar to see Todd. I explained all that the bar had said to me and what the manager was planning to do and how different it was going to be. In my opinion, I didn't think it was going to get far.

"The problem is, Todd, if I don't take the contract on, someone else will and then you'll have full-on rivalry. It's a case of better the devil you know than the one you don't. But if you're happy with me taking it on rather than someone else, I can make some suggestions to make things work better in your favour."

"Like?" he asked.

"Like, you get to choose which girls off our list that you want exclusively at your bar and I will make sure they don't ever get a shift over the road."

"Okay right, so I want…" and listed a good 10 or so girls he knew had regulars or who the guys specifically liked. I jotted them down.

"Secondly, it's going to be a topless-only night every other Tuesday. If you really don't like the idea of the squaddies going there and spending their money (both bars were near a Barracks), run a blue night on the same Tuesday – maybe go the full opposite to what they do?"

"That's an excellent idea!" And I could already see the cogs turning in his head.

"Right, so I'll get back to their manager when I get home and tell them I'll take it on then, okay?"

"Yep, no problem, thanks for being straight and keeping me in the loop."

Two weeks came and I started the contract at the bar with three of my girls and the pub having a "house girl" who would be there every time they ran the night. I guess that was to double confirm there would always be a girl working there if any of mine were no-shows. It wasn't busy but ended up being semi-steady and was a bearable night for the local girls. For anyone having to pay out travel fees to get there though, it wouldn't have been worth their while.

Todd informed me the Cellar bar was making great money that night:

"Running a blue show twice a month on Tuesdays was a great idea."

He knew I was looking out for his bar, as those house fees went to the other agent so I never gained from it. And because I didn't earn from it, the other bar would never know the idea came from me.

Everyone was happy. The non-blue girls were happy to get more work on a day when I had no other contracts offered. The bar made a little extra money with girls there, although not as much as they had anticipated (I did warn them!) And the blue girls and Todd were making great money over the road.

With that contract set in stone fortnightly and proudly pinning the venue beside the day of the week on my noticeboard, I took a step back. In just over a year and a half, I had permanent contracts on

A Conflict Of Interest

Sundays (two of them), Tuesdays (fortnightly), Thursdays and Fridays, along with ad-hoc venues and events. I was pretty happy with that. As I stared at it and smiled, my phone rang. I wondered who was calling me so late at night. It was Abel.

> "Holly, we need girls to go to Portugal as soon as possible, the owner is really desperate for them...."

28
LIE UPON LIE

Rather than ask Abel a bunch of questions to ask the Club owner in Portugal, he gave me Timmy's number to liaise with him directly.

"Hi Timmy, it's Holly, the UK agent who works with Abel."

"Hi, how are you?" he asked in a friendly voice.

"Great, thanks! I have a few questions as I want to make sure I send you the right girls – I've had issues before with venues giving off mixed signals, or the wrong girls for their club arriving and I obviously don't want to waste your time or theirs."

"Sure, fire away."

Timmy explained to me he ideally wanted girls to stay for a minimum of two weeks and he said he would offer free accommodation to them, in a "dancer" house. In the well-established, busy club, dances were offered to clientele as well as selling champagne and the fees were a 50-50 split of earnings. He also provided dancers for private parties, like stripograms for birthdays and stag parties; girls could work those on some nights if they wished and return to the club later (they would have a member of security with them at all times so they would be safe). He didn't necessarily want dancers of any particular look; he was open to all types and sizes as long as they worked hard. Everything seemed pretty straightforward and after jotting down the notes I texted all the girls on my books:

> "Dance contracts in Portugal available (minimum two weeks). Send me your email address for more details."

About five girls asked for more information, and after forwarding on, two said they wanted to go – Charlie and Annika. They had been working for me since I started the agency and were hard workers. Charlie had to hold out for a week or so, while Annika was happy to travel there on her own in the next few days.

I spoke to Timmy and told him when to expect Annika. He gave me details for her to get a bus from the airport to the house. Annika said she would keep me posted when she reached her final destination.

Annika texted me from the house and said there were four girls staying there who didn't speak much English. They were Russian and Eastern European. She said the sheets on her bed were all dirty. I texted Tommy, who sorted out the issue and apologised and said the cleaners hadn't yet been in. Annika rested for the duration of the afternoon and was picked up that night by a security-guy-come-driver along with the other girls and taken to the club.

Informing me the club was pretty dead, Annika, being one of my most professional girls, still gave it her all on stage. We assumed perhaps it was dead because it was a Monday and as dancers who have worked for years, we generally expected the earlier part of the week to be quieter. From what I gathered, the other girls were pretty new and looked at her in awe as she took to the stage.

Timmy also called me that night:

"Annika is amazing! Thank you for sending me such a skilled worker!"

"No problem" I said, "Like I said before, I have great girls and can always send the right ones once I know what a contract entails."

Annika spent some time sitting with Timmy that night when there were no customers to talk to and discovered the club had only been open a couple of months.

"*Well established*" – lie number one.

She tried to give him some suggestions as to how to make the club busier, like sending girls out earlier on in the night and handing out flyers. He took it on board, and immediately took a shine to Annika because she was so helpful, as well as beautiful.

She texted me that night to tell me about how long the club had been open, knowing that I wouldn't have lied to her and that he had misinformed me in order to get girls working there.

"Hopefully it will get busier, but tell Charlie not to come over yet, in case it stays bad. We don't want two dancers losing out."

"Will do, sorry he's lied to me, I'm pretty pissed off right now but let's hope it picks up towards the weekend."

I called Charlie and told her about Annika's findings and that it would be best she didn't book a ticket yet. She thanked me for telling her and told me to keep her posted if things happened to change.

The second night was the same, with no customers.

"*Busy club*" – lie number two.

Come the third night, a girl was told there was a job for her at a private event, and a member of security took her. Sitting with Timmy again, Annika asked if she could go to one if there was guaranteed money, as she also had stripogram experience, but he refused her and made the excuse:

"I need you here for when customers show as you are the best girl here, a talented dancer, a great talker as you speak the best English, and very beautiful."

He smiled and spoke to her a lot differently than he did the other girls. With them he took a darker tone.

Once the night ended and the dancers were dropped back at the house, the girl who had been sent to the private party was also dropped back and went straight to the room she shared with Annika. She was shaking and crying. She sat on the edge of her bed, staring at the floor. She wouldn't tell Annika what was wrong or what had happened. The security guy who dropped her off, and the guy who dropped off the other dancers, "collected" another girl from her room, who was resisting going, and they dragged her into one of the cars and drove off. She returned the following day, her arms and legs covered in bruises.

> *"Dancers would have a member of security with them at all times so they would be safe"* – lie number three.

Whilst obvious what was happening to these girls, neither Annika or I asked questions. Ignorance was the best way forward. We knew Annika needed to get out, but no money could be wired to her as the house wasn't near anywhere to collect any money.

> "My boyfriend can book me a ticket to fly back, but I need to play the long game here," she said. "I'm pretty sure Timmy's adoration is what's saved me from being sent to the private parties. He thinks he's in with a chance with me so he won't allow me to be manhandled by anyone else. Give me a couple of days and I'll get this sorted. I have a plan. If Timmy calls you, pretend you don't know anything about the girls and the private jobs."

I was worried for Annika, but out of all the girls who worked for me, I knew she could look after herself the best and I trusted her when she said she had a plan to get out.

During the next couple of days, Annika talked to Timmy more, in between the very few dances and drinks she managed to sell with the small number of customers the club attracted. She read him right, Timmy did have a thing for her, so she did what she said and played the long game. She made out she had a thing for him too, but if they were going to be together it would only be fair that she flew back to England to end things with her boyfriend face to face.

> "It's the right thing to do," she insisted; "that's how I'd expect someone to end things with me if I'd been with them for so long."

Being "so honest and upfront" only made Timmy more attracted to her. He agreed, and gave her cash for a flight so she could book something at the airport.

> "Don't worry about completing the two weeks here," he said. "Go tomorrow and get it sorted so you can come back as soon as you can and we can be together."

"I'm not going to give you my number yet as I don't want you calling when I'm with my boyfriend. It could cause problems and I don't want him knowing I'm finishing things because I've met you. Give Holly a call in a couple of days and she will give you my number. I'll tell her it's okay."

"No problem, if you gave me your number now, I think I wouldn't be able to stop myself from calling you, so you're right. I'll call Holly."

Annika texted me the next day:

"I'm at the airport, I'll ring you when I land."

Breathing a sigh of relief, I kept my phone with me at all times as I didn't want to miss the call from her.

Three hours later, she called, slightly teary.

"I'm back. Oh my God, I can't believe I managed to get out!"

She told me how she played Timmy to get home and that her boyfriend booked her a flight from his end. With the money Timmy gave her, she got a bus and tried to get two of the other dancers to come with her to the airport to get out. One was so terrified she wouldn't leave the house. The other girl got as far as the bus stop with Annika, and when the bus came she froze and couldn't get on:

"He will come find me," she trembled. "You go, I'll stay."

Annika tried to convince her everything would be okay, but to no avail. She felt helpless but knew she had to leave regardless. It was horrible how much power Timmy had over these girls, for them to think they would not be safe wherever they went. And we all knew they were far from safe where they were. Who knew what would happen to them long-term.

"I'm so sorry, Annika." I apologised excessively.

"It's okay, it's not your fault. You had all the information he gave you and you forwarded it on. I'm just glad Charlie didn't come as it would have been more difficult getting two of us out. He'd wonder why she was leaving at the same time."

I rang Abel and told him what happened. He couldn't believe what he was hearing.

"I'm not sending girls to any more of these contracts unless you or I have been to the clubs ourselves. She's lucky she got out, Abel. I'm not putting my girls in danger."

"I'm sorry, Holly, and I agree. Do you want me to ring Timmy?"

"No, don't worry, I'm sure I'll be hearing from him soon."

He rang three days later, like Annika told him to. He spoke in his usual, happy voice, asking for Annika's number.

"She's not leaving her boyfriend, and she's not coming back to Portugal. I don't appreciate being lied to. Don't *ever* contact me or Abel again... Your club isn't safe and you're a glorified pimp. If I find you contact any other agents over here, I will name and shame you and contact the authorities."

I hung up the phone.

I felt like I'd let Annika down. I couldn't undo what she had been through, so I offered her all cancellation shifts for the next week and extra shifts for the next two weeks to make up for it.

England may not always be the busiest of places to work, but at least we knew where we stood.

29
SPLOSH

The videographer for whom I'd filmed the girl-on-girl wrestling I worked for (and who had the custom tit slapper fantasist) asked me if I had a girl on my books who would like to come and do some scenes. Out of my folder, he picked Annika to work for him with another girl he had used before. This time, he had hired out seats around the mats for guys to watch the girls fight, so unlike when Alicia and I kept being told to stop laughing and having to refilm, it had to be "staged" perfectly for the live event. The girls would discuss behind the scenes what moves to do and who would win, but there was to be no penetration, unlike the heavier girl-on-girl one that I'd taken part in previously. This was a lot more thigh clenching, boob suffocating, and pinning girls down with their full bodies.

Funnily enough, at the time of booking, *another* "wrestling" company contacted me to ask if they could look at the girls on my books. Their wrestling was slightly different; the girls would wrestle a guy (although the guys were to act weak and submissive, rather than *actually* wrestle the girls), and there would be a lot of face-sitting involved on the guy (the girls being clothed, and encouraged to wear two pairs of larger briefs, to avoid accidents where bits of body parts might "pop out"). I suggested he pick out the girls he liked the look of and then I would approach them to see if they would be happy doing it.

A couple of the girls he picked said no, as they did not want to be known for working with men at all (even if the men were fully clothed). They didn't want the stigma of some narrow-minded people more than likely saying "Oh you're filming with men now?" and assume there would be an uncensored video somewhere of them with all their clothes off.

The other girl he picked was Annika. She was popular, probably because she had a dominant look; being fairly tall and having big boobs too helped emanate that look. She was interested and went down a storm for that company and they ended up requesting her several times over as more and more guys wanted to submit to Annika. And she loved working for them, much more than the spectator wrestling sessions from the other videographer.

I was pleased after the Portugal shit storm that Annika was immediately getting more bookings. She ended up making more money than she probably would have done had she stayed out there. And at least she was safe and the only façade she had to put on was when she was wrestling. I also had a full day's work booked for five dancers in my pole studio and I invited Annika along to work on that.

We – I had booked myself in for this job too – had to pole-dance solo in five different outfits, to whatever music we wanted to whilst being filmed. There was a lot of sitting around at Granddad's house, which Granddad quite liked as it meant he had a day's worth of company, and pretty girls. Claire also worked that day and she knew Granddad quite well so sat and chatted to him loudly and clearly as she was used to talking to him. Girls would walk out of the studio after performing to their song, completely forgetting Granddad was there and he never even batted an eyelid. It seemed nakedness never bothered him. He'd just ask:

"Do you want another cup of tea?" as if they were fully clothed and the girls felt really comfortable.

"Usually the older men in the camera clubs do nothing but ogle" one of them said; "this makes a pleasant change. I'd happily come and work here again! YES PLEASE," she shouted to Granddad, "milk, one sugar."

Granddad also liked to dote on people and it made him feel useful.

I was yielding better monetarily from modelling commissions now in addition to dancer's fees, and still booking myself in as and when for both. Whilst requests like wrestling were left to girls like Annika, I was offered a shoot for another very specialised fetish – called "Splosh."

Splosh, also known as WAM (Wet and Messy) is a fetish whereby seeing someone covered in food arouses a client. I don't get it. I understand most fetishes, even if they're not to my liking, but apparently the fixation is based either on the visual appeal of the textures, or the idea of sensations of wet and messy substances, mostly against bare skin. Scenes can be shot fully nude, some in bikinis, others wearing clothes and covering them or models pouring food into their clothing so it oozes out. Sometimes scenes would even be of girls sitting on piles of various foodstuffs.

My friend Ariana was the first girl I knew that had done a lot of filming in this field, and she was happy sitting in a bath and covering herself in cold custard or cold baked beans for the right amount of money. Personally, I would have heaved – I find the smell of cold baked beans vile!

She had recently done a shoot involving custard pie fights with another girl and she recommended me to the photographer. Thankfully, these custard pies were to be made with shaving foam and food colouring, so I accepted the position of pie thrower.

I drove down to the Sussex studio one morning, where the photographer/videographer informed me this was for a specific model's website that involved *just* splosh photos and movies, and it had gained quite a bit of traction. The model, Sam, on some days shot solo films, throwing food over herself, "accidentally" getting messy, for example in kitchen scenes cooking and baking, and other days filmed with other models. She would get emails from her fans saying:

> "I really liked you in scene "x" but next time can you make sure you get more food in your/her face please?" Or "We want more down the top/on the boobs."

They were really engaged in what they were subscribing to.

I took three outfits with me; Sam requested I take bikini sets, short skirts, and cute looking tops, and of course a towel, as obviously we would need to get cleaned up and change in between each shoot, *and* reapply our make-up.

I don't think the subscribers were too bothered about storylines, but we had to start off with some sort of plot in order to warrant getting pied. The photographer whipped up the pies in between each scene, and cleaned off our clothes to the best of his ability before they would stain with the food colouring. He also needed to clean the studio area in case any foam had flown off the plates and got onto the floor or the walls.

One scene was a staged argument, which began with Sam covering the top of my head with a pie, the foam hanging off my hair either side of my head, and me retaliating with a pie in each hand and aiming straight for her boobs. There were big pauses in between, as if we were really shocked it had happened. Sam came back at my boobs with another two pies, and I finished by smacking her in the face with a pie and twisting it, before allowing the paper plate to fall to the floor, leaving Sam to scrape the pie away from her eyes with her fingers and shaking away residue. At least the lingering pie smells in our hair were fresh and clean from the shaving foam, rather than a milky smell from real cream.

In another scene, Sam was hiding around a corner in stealth mode, whilst I innocently walked along minding my own business, in a very over-exaggerated way, until she popped out from around the corner and hit me directly in the face with a pie. I did the eye wiping thing as Sam had done before, as the subscribers liked to see nothing more than a face full of pie and two eye holes blinking away in shock and a mouth hole. I spun round, bent over to pretend I was wiping more away from my eye, and Sam smacked another pie up my short skirt onto my butt, when the cameraman then cued an upskirt foam pie shot.

This was pure slapstick comedy, a bit like some of the old black and white movies. Perhaps this fetish catered to an older subscriber crowd that used to enjoy those films, but since the subscribers were anonymous, we would never know. Much like when I posed for the petticoat pictures with Crystal.

Scene three was a Happy Birthday request. I had seen girls sing happy birthday before and then sit on a cake at the end. But one of Sam's fans had asked if we could sing happy birthday and then sit on some pies. We decided to take it to a slightly higher level. Wearing just our thongs, with all the pies ready, scattered around us, we began, taking a line each to sing:

(Sam) "Happy birthday, to you…"
She slapped two plates worth of pie onto her boobs.

SPLOSH

(Me)   "...Happy birthday to you..."

I copied Sam and did the same with two pies to myself.

(Both of us) "Happy birthday dear Robert..."

We sat on a pie each, the foam puffing up in the air and then ended the song -

"...Happy birthday to youuuuuuu!"

Slapping a pie in each other's face, leaving the plates there waiting for them to slide and drop onto the floor.

We heard the beep of the camera as the videographer switched it off:

"Good work, girls, we've got some good footage today."

Although messy, I did enjoy the job. It made a nice change doing something fun and not too serious and both Sam and the cameraman were great to work with.

I cleaned myself up and scraped back my fresh smelling hair, putting it in a ponytail. The ends had all stuck together in clumps and I would have looked ridiculous going home with it down. I took the money from the videographer and said if they ever needed me again to get in touch, and I texted Ariana to thank her.

The roads were clear so I had time to detour to Granddad's on the way home for a cup of tea. He was sitting in his tub chair by the coffee table, watching the world go by out of the window. He was pleased to see me; he hadn't done much that day as he was tired (sometimes the tinnitus was too much for him) and I told him I'd just finished my modelling job in Sussex. We chatted about what else I was up to that week – I would always write down on a piece of paper where I was working for the week and my hours, so that if Granddad needed anything and he knew I was not in the area, he could ring Martin instead, who was only about 20 minutes away. Martin and I, although separated, were still fantastic friends and he still saw us as family, and I still considered him and his family as part of mine.

I knew he would be over tomorrow as he always visited Granddad on Wednesday nights straight after work for dinner. After drinking my tea, I cleared away our cups and said:

"I'm having the day off tomorrow and I know Martin's over for dinner, so I'll pop in and see you Thursday."

"Thursday?" he repeated. I nodded. "Okay bab."

SPLOSH

I gave him a hug and a kiss goodbye and I left for home.

Unbeknown to me, that was the last time we would ever speak to one another.

30
GRANDDAD

I had decided to stay at home on my day off and chill out, but the strangest things began to happen to me from that Wednesday morning, which to this day I can't explain.

I switched on my phone at 9.15am even though I was still lying in bed enjoying the comfort of my duvet wrapped around me. Usually, if I was ever having a day off, and no girls were working on one of my contracts that day, I wouldn't switch my phone on until later. But I felt something was "telling me" or "guiding me" to switch it on early. As I did, it bleeped; answer phone message. It was left at 9am by Alex, one of Granddad's closest friends, whom Granddad looked upon like a son. He would always call in to see Granddad for coffee a couple of times a week on his way to work at his shop.

"I've just called in to see Jim and he's not answering and the key's not in the door. Can you go check on him when you get this message."

Granddad was always up by around 6.30am and once dressed without fail, he would put the key in the door – one of his old-fashioned ways. The door to his property didn't directly face the road, so it was fairly safe to have the key in without random passers-by seeing it. I rose from my bed, got washed and dressed and drove to Granddad's.

Still no key in the door so I used mine, but the chain was still on, so it only opened so far. They say that when someone gets angry or stressed, they can receive a sudden burst of adrenaline, enabling them to become extremely strong for seconds or minutes. Somehow, I managed to get the chain off the door that day and get into the house. I was later questioned about how I did it. I didn't know the answer to that question then, and I still don't know now.

Granddad was lying in bed snoring. "Bless him" I thought, smiling. He must have needed that lie in. I shouted "Granddad" loudly so he could hear over his tinnitus. Nothing. Next, I stroked his hair so I wouldn't scare him when he woke up to see me standing over him. He continued to snore loudly. No change. My smile disappeared. I tapped him on the shoulder.

"Granddad. Granddad!"

Nothing but snoring. Panic set in. I shook him by the shoulders but he continued to snore. I ran to the phone to call the Doctor and tell them that I couldn't wake him up.

"Ring emergency services" said the Receptionist.

"999 which service do you require" said the Operator

"Ambulance, please" I said, shaking and crying

"Connecting you..."

"Hello, can I help you?"

"Yes, please send an ambulance I can't wake my Granddad up" still shaking.

"Ok, how old is he?"

"79"

"Is he breathing?" said the voice at the end of the phone

"Yes"

"Is he laying on his back?"

"Yes, he sounds like he's snoring, but I can't wake him up."

"Ok there's an ambulance on its way, my love. In the meantime I'm going to have to ask you to make sure his airway is unblocked"

The phone I was calling on was in the living room and was corded. Everything I did, I had to keep running into the bedroom and back to the phone.

"I need you to check he isn't swallowing his tongue and then if he isn't to then remove the pillow from under him and lift his chin and tilt his head back."

I put my fingers in his mouth. His airway was clear. His head seemed so heavy. It was hard for me to get the pillow out from underneath him.

"Okay, I've done that" I told the voice.

Next, she asked me some medical questions:

"Is he diabetic?"

"Yes" I replied "Type 2."

"Ok, my love, he may have gone into a diabetic coma. The ambulance should be with you shortly"

I hung up the phone and went back into Granddad's room, kneeled down beside the bed and held his hand.

"It's ok, Granddad" I said, "It's just your diabetes, you'll be ok when they get you to the hospital."

I rang Martin at work to tell him an ambulance was coming. The ambulance car arrived first on the scene as it was nearer to Granddad's than the van. She started to do checks. Blood pressure.

"His blood pressure has always been excellent," I told her. It seemed fine.

Martin must have driven so fast because he reached Granddad's by the time the ambulance van showed up. The ambulance driver and other Medic arrived to see what the progress was. I explained that he was diabetic. One of them did a finger prick test for his blood sugar. Normal.

"But the lady on the phone said it was probably a diabetic coma?"

"It's not, love" the Medic said to me

"So what is it?" I asked, teary and shaking

"His arm is really cold; could be a stroke. We need to get him in the ambulance and take him to A&E."

I still wanted to believe that he was in a diabetic coma, but he wasn't.

The stretcher wouldn't fit in the house around the tight corner of the fence and the high steps, so the paramedics had to strap Granddad in a chair. His long white hair was a mess. They wheeled him down the driveway onto the main road to the ambulance. I was so worried for him; worried he would worry about people looking at him as they drove by. I hated it because I knew he would have hated it. They got him into the back and put him on the stretcher. I travelled in the ambulance with him and Martin followed behind in his car.

Granddad was pushing his arm against the Medic standing next to him, like he was pushing him away.

"That's a good sign" the Medic said to me, but by this time nothing would ease the worries I had.

The siren of the ambulance seemed so loud from the inside, echoing around the contained space. It felt like forever to get to the hospital. Upon arrival they wheeled him into the A&E ward and gave me paperwork to hand over at reception. Apparently I was standing too close to the inpatient standing at the front of the reception desk who proceeded to snap at me and tell me I should stand back behind the line, even though the paramedics stood me beside him, and being in the foggy cloud I was, I just did what they said. Today was *not* the day to pick a fight with me. I didn't care less what was wrong with the person being seen by the receptionist. All I wanted to do was hand over the paperwork and go back and find Granddad. After snapping at the rude patient they shut up and realised I would not be moved until the other receptionist came forward and dealt with my details. They were standing, walking and talking. Compared to Granddad, they were fine.

Granddad was given a room. They were checking his eyes, blood pressure, bloods and doing all sorts of other tests. They were asking me questions such as what medication is he on and I listed them. They asked me if my Granddad was suicidal and if I'd thought he may have taken an overdose. I looked at them bewildered and shook my head:

"No, he wouldn't have taken an overdose."

By this stage Martin's Mum showed up as Martin had called her en route. There were three of us sitting around Granddad in a room, with Nurses and Doctors buzzing in and out, with no one giving us any answers. I felt useless just sitting there and doing nothing else. I needed a cigarette. I went outside. I rang Alex to tell him that I was at the hospital and to thank him for ringing me. If I hadn't, Granddad wasn't expecting to see anyone else that day until Martin that evening for dinner. Alex was upset and told me to keep him posted. I rang Claire in tears. She also never used to switch her phone on until she got out of bed but for some reason, decided to switch it on earlier that day. She was in London working on the girl channels and said she would come down as soon as she could find someone to drive her.

No cigarette lighter in my bag. Typical. No one around to ask for one either. I went back in.

The Doctors and Nurses were doing the same tests as before, nothing looked any different and I was starting to get irritated.

"So what's happening?" I blurted out. "Have you found *anything*?"

344

"We have eliminated everything else, so we think he may have had a stroke" replied the Doctor.

"Ok, so what can you do?" I asked.

There was a pause from him. A long pause, too long. And within that pause I could hear bleeps of monitors; deafening bleeps, and I wondered if Granddad could hear them over his tinnitus.

I took the Doctor's silence as a bad sign. I asked the dreaded question on mine, Martin's and Mum's lips.

"Is my Granddad going to die?" The Doctor and Nurse looked at me:

"Well, he's been unconscious for a while, so the lack of oxygen..."

I interrupted, and gritted my teeth:

"I said, *is* my Granddad going to die?" I just wanted an answer to my question.

"Yes." the Doctor replied.

Grand Dad

I sat still. Tears clouded my eyes; my breathing became shallow. Martin and his Mum also started to cry. The bright room became too claustrophobic for me. I had to get up, had to get out. I needed to start ringing people. People I knew would want to know. Auntie Dee, Uncle Gerald, Alex, Claire, his friend Dave and nieces and nephews who adored Granddad. I had to do something because doing nothing was getting to me and making me feel helpless. And still there was no one around who had a light for my cigarette. I was gasping. A Nurse walked by me:

"Excuse me, do you have a light?" I asked.

"No, I don't smoke, I'm a Nurse"

"Oh sorry, yes because I suppose you don't drink either, what with being a Nurse" I said sarcastically.

She smiled "Fair comment".

Still no light though. For the love of God does anyone have a light right now?! It was as if the hospital grounds were deserted of smokers. Still without being able to light my menthol nicotine stick, I went back inside the hospital after making some of the calls.

We sat in the family room, waiting. I had no clue what for.

346

The Doctor wanted to speak to me again:

"If your Granddad stops breathing, do you want us to resuscitate him?"

I looked at them puzzled, wondering what sort of stupid question that really was.

"*Of course* I want you to resuscitate him!" I said firmly. "I want him to live!"

"Please bear in mind, that if we do resuscitate him and he does actually come round, it's more than likely that he will be severely brain damaged as he's been unconscious for some time now."

I couldn't believe what they were asking me to do. In my eyes, they didn't think it was worth even trying to revive him. He was *my* Granddad. He had been like a father to me most of my life, but as if he was nothing, the Doctor expected me to give them an answer with such a quick response and to make me decide whether he lived or died. I did not want to play the part of Death; holding an hourglass, waiting for the last grain of sand to fall. I couldn't deal with all these questions anymore. I went outside again.

Grand Dad

I rang Auntie Dee again and told her what they had said. She put it into perspective:

> "Think about it, Babby. Do you think if Granddad woke up that he would want to live, with the inability to do anything or to have other people do things for him?"

With the phone to my ear and my lip trembling, my eyes filled with tears again.

> "No," I replied, "No he wouldn't."

Hanging up from the phone, I gathered myself and walked back in to see the Doctor. I took some deep breaths as I looked at him:

> "With regard to your question earlier," I took another deep breath, "the answer is no, I think it's best you don't resuscitate him."

The Doctor nodded in agreement and wrote "DNR" on Granddad's notes on the clipboard. "DO NOT RESUSCITATE"

> "We'll make him comfortable so he won't be suffering."

I wondered how they would even know if he was comfortable or not suffering. I knew hospital beds were hard; he spent a lot of time in one years ago when he was bedridden from a trapped nerve in his spine. I also know if he had the choice, he would want to die at home, as Nanny had died before him when I was a little girl. He held her as she died and Granddad had said to me she had shed a tear in his arms in her final moments.

They moved him out of the intensive care unit and put him in a curtained cubicle in A&E, and only three were allowed at a time by his bedside. Sitting, waiting, was all we could do. I sat next to him. How would he know I was there? He was deaf most of the time so I couldn't talk to him normally like you would most coma patients, when Doctors and Nurses usually tell you they can hear you. So I held his hand. He used to like his hair being played with and stroked, ever since his Mother used to do it when he was a little boy. So I stroked his head whilst he breathed through his tube. A song played over the radio in the background; the lyrics stood out as it was about someone pretending that someone they loved was still there with them. My tears were unstoppable. My face was sore and my eyes swollen as I sat in the confined curtained room with him.

Gradually, more friends and family arrived. Granddad's other best friend Dave and his wife, Auntie Dee, and Claire, who arrived on a road sweeper; she said she'd get to the hospital from London somehow and she did. We had to laugh. That was sheer determination on her part. Claire came with me to get a coffee. I hadn't had a drink all day because I wanted to stay close to Granddad. Halfway through walking to the coffee shop, Martin had run to find us.

"Lydia's here, you should come; she's in a bit of a state." She had turned up and instead of the Nurses showing her to the family room where everyone else was, they took her straight to Granddad's bed without preparing her for what she would see. By the time I got back to the cubicle, she was in pieces. Crying uncontrollably and nodding in belief, she said:

"He'll be ok, they just have to wait for him to wake up."

"He's not going to wake up, honey" I replied.

Lydia's head fell onto my chest and I held her. She seemed so vulnerable.

"But he *might* wake up, he's breathing fine; he's strong, we know he's strong and…"

"Look at me, honey", I looked her in the eyes and held her face "he won't wake up, he's been unconscious for too long. He's going to die. Sometime soon."

She cried and cried, and that in turn made *me* cry again; but I had to be in control. We walked her into the family room. The others took it in turns to sit with Granddad and say their goodbyes.

We were informed that they were going to put Granddad on a ward where he would be even more "comfortable". I knew they meant "where he will die". They took him off the ventilator so he had no help breathing and he would eventually stop, but his breathing still seemed so strong without it.

"We're moving him to the elderly ward" said one of the Nurses.

Granddad may have been 79 years old, but he was normally very active and most people would forget how old he really was; including Claire and I, who immediately said to the Nurse:

"But he's not old! Why does he have to go on the elderly ward?"

Grand Dad

I guess to them it didn't matter what he was to us. He just needed a place to slip away and someone else needed the cubicle in A&E. We followed the porter who moved him.

I sat one side of him, Auntie Dee the other. I placed a handkerchief in his hand so he had something to hold that was familiar; Granddad always had a handkerchief. I felt so useless just sitting there. I gave Dee one of Granddad's other hankies I had on me to wipe her tears, and told her she could keep it. She smiled:

"Thank you," she said. It was a comfort to her.

Another hour passed. It was getting late. Dee decided to leave. I gave her a hug, looked at Granddad over her shoulder and decided

"I'm leaving too."

I couldn't sit with him any longer, unable to do anything. I didn't want to hear the other people on the ward talking to each other and going about their day as if everything was okay. I gave him a kiss, stroked his head again and said goodbye and promised I'd be back tomorrow. Claire came with me to stay the night.

Once we were back at my flat, I made a few more calls and emails to let more people know the situation and which ward he was in, should anybody want to visit him whilst he was still alive. Claire was ironing as a distraction. Cleaning and tidying were always her go to if she needed to be distracted. I guess we went to bed a little after midnight. Claire stayed on the futon in the lounge, I slept in my room. Well, at least, I tried to. The night was unsettling. Unexplained things were occurring around me. I was awoken by something lying beside me on my pillow. I could feel it. The weight was like a person. I turned to look and it vanished. Orbs of light appeared and floated around my room. I had always believed in spirits and life after death, for years on and off I'd attended spiritualist churches and been told I had a "gift", but I always chose not to use it. I had dabbled in tarot cards but that was as far as I had got.

I chose to stay in my room even though I had insomnia as I didn't want to wake up Claire. I drifted in and out of sleep all night, wanting to go back and see Granddad, but telling myself not to. I didn't want to see him take his last breath. It would be too final for me. As dawn broke, the birds started to sing outside and I finally drifted off. When I woke up again, I checked the time on my phone: 6.40am. I laid there wondering what time we should go back to see him, but ten minutes later the hospital rang:

"Your Granddad passed away at 6.40 this morning. Would you like to come and see him?"

Grand Dad

"I'll be straight there" I answered.

I knew it was going to happen but didn't think it would be this soon. I thought I could have gone to see him again and sit with him some more before he died. Whilst getting dressed, I rang Auntie Dee. She cried so hard down the phone:

"I prayed and prayed he wouldn't suffer and they would take him away quickly."

Tears ran down my face.

"Do you want to come with us?"

But Dee wanted to remember him as he was before he fell ill. Martin drove to mine to take Claire and I to the hospital.

"You didn't sleep well, did you?" Claire asked me.

"Not really"

"I heard you pacing up and down in the corridor during the night."

I hadn't left my room. Claire had said she'd heard someone walking up and down, as if the person was wearing trousers or jeans that were chaffing. With that, the orbs and the person lying next to me, I wondered what it had all meant. I'd like to think it was someone looking out for me, or Granddad already around me because he was slowly slipping away.

We arrived at the hospital and a Doctor met with us.

"Well, as you know, your Granddad died this morning."

The Doctor was smiling. *Why* was he smiling? I had been given the worst news in the world and this Doctor was not helping. I couldn't say anything, I was too upset.

"He's in the ward if you want to go and see him."

I went in on my own. Claire didn't want to go in and waited for me in the waiting room. Martin waited for me to go in first. I walked into the ward and drew back the curtain. I had never seen anyone dead before. I started to sob. His mouth had fallen to one side and he was still clutching the handkerchief I had put in his hand the night before. He didn't look like my Granddad anymore. I stroked his hair once more and gave him a kiss on the forehead. I stepped outside and let Martin in to say his goodbyes.

Grand Dad

As we drove back to Granddad's house in silence I sat in disbelief. I never once thought about life without my Granddad. My weekly routine always involved popping in to see him and having a cup of tea. What was I supposed to do now? Who was I going to love and who was going to love me?

"I have no one now," I thought to myself. "I'm alone."

The rest of the day consisted of sitting round the dining table at Granddad's house, drinking tea, smoking, receiving visitors, hugging one another, crying, drinking more tea, reminiscing and smoking more cigarettes. We didn't know what else we could do. As the day progressed, people arrived, people left. And then I went home and tried to sleep.

My eyes were puffy, my nose sore from constantly blowing it. I didn't want to sleep in my bedroom so fell asleep on the futon in the living room with the television on. I'd hoped that if I woke up in the morning, none of it would be true. Granddad would be very much alive and it was all just a nightmare that I'd dreamed about. But of course, the morning came and I was still living the nightmare, which was now my reality.

From getting Granddad's Death Certificate to arranging the funeral, it was a never-ending cycle of unhappiness. Phone calls telling people what had happened, the repetition of how it happened, trying to run my agency and still dance and make money whilst it was all going on, *and* trying to look happy at work. It took it out of me. I put on a brave face, inside I was cracking, but wouldn't let anyone see.

The funeral wasn't until 15 days later. It seemed like a lifetime to wait to put him to rest. The day before his burial, I arranged to go and see him in the Chapel of Rest at the Funeral Directors, which was directly opposite my flat. I could see the building from my living room.

The lady in the Funeral Director's led me into the room he was in. I was so nervous to see him again. She said I could stay in there for as long as I wanted to, then she left me with him.

There he was. Lying in the coffin in the suit he wore to my Nanny's funeral. He looked really smart. He looked so still, so peaceful and as if he was smiling, as the corners of his mouth were slightly up. I was told before coming in that I was allowed to put things in the coffin if I wanted to, things I thought he would like to be buried with. I talked to him whilst I reached in the bag I'd brought with me and pulled them out one by one. His teddy bear that someone had knitted for him years ago; which Granddad called Bert; pictures of me, Nanny and Martin; his amethyst crystal that he slept with under his pillow, that was supposed to help with his tinnitus. I put them all in. And then I touched him. He was so cold. So icy cold. I will never forget how that felt on my hand. The coldness ran up my hand into my arm. It was a shock. It shouldn't have been, but I guess it hadn't crossed my mind that he'd been "persevered" somehow for the last two weeks. I sat in the chair beside him and cried. Cried because I missed him. I wanted to cuddle him but he would just be cold and wouldn't feel like my Granddad anymore. I sat and talked to him some more. I told him about the funeral and the arrangements I'd made, and how much I'd been missing him. When I felt that I couldn't stay any longer, I told him I loved him and I left the building and walked back across the road to my flat.

The day was long. I spent it sorting through photographs to put up in the pub at the wake. Photos of Granddad with me and other members of the family. I made food for the wake. I did basically anything that would keep me busy and make the day go quicker. I picked up Claire from work that evening in London as she wanted to stay at mine the night before and help with preparations.

After lying awake in bed again for what seemed like hours, I finally fell asleep for a bit. It wasn't long before my alarm went off and it was time to get up. Claire did my hair for me; I wanted to look my best for my Granddad. He always liked me to look smart.

The funeral procession and Granddad were to leave from his house. Martin, his Mum, Lydia, Claire and I waited for him to arrive. Two dapple grey horses with plumes led the procession with Granddad in the carriage, followed by a hearse with the flowers, and then the car for us. We all walked down the driveway. We looked at the flowers in the car and I stroked the horses, as if to say thank you for taking Granddad to his final resting place. Granddad's Dad, my Great Grandfather, used to keep horses, so Granddad had a love for them and he had said in the past that he wanted a horse drawn carriage to take him to his funeral. The funeral procession began and we slowed down the traffic. As we passed the café at the bottom of the road (Granddad's favourite eating place), the staff were standing outside paying their respects and one of the ladies was crying. It was touching to know he was missed.

We pulled up at the Churchyard. Crowds of people walked into the Church to wait for us. Friends, family, acquaintances of Granddad, my old school friends and dancers who I worked with who Granddad had met had come along to pay their respects. The old flint Church was full to the brim. I sat at the front with Claire and Lydia, Martin and his Mum sat behind us.

We stood up and the pawn bearers carried him in. We were all crying. I was in pieces. I had written down the eulogy in case I was too upset to read it out and the Priest in Charge could take over. But

I managed to find the strength to read it all out loud myself. It took time, but I read it, along with the poem "Death is nothing at all" by Henry Scott Holland.

The song that played for him was "Unchained Melody" by the Righteous Brothers. He used to love that song, and he loved it when it made a comeback in the charts in the '90s on a film soundtrack. Just sitting there listening to it, listening to the words, was perturbing. All I could do was hold my friends' hands whilst the tears streamed down my face. Claire had marks where her foundation had run off with her tears. Most of my dancer friends had never been to a funeral before, so it was overwhelming for them too.

The final song we had was a hymn for us to all sing; Jerusalem. It was Granddad's favourite, and it was played at my wedding because Granddad liked it so much. The Church may have been full but it was sung with poor effort by everyone. I guess it was hard to sing because we were all so melancholy.

It was time for the burial and Granddad was carried out of the Church. He was led by a Bagpiper; the final thing Granddad had said he wanted when he died. The piper played "Amazing Grace". We followed behind up to the graveside. The piper stood on the windy hill and continued to play until everyone reached the final resting place. Granddad was to be buried with my Nanny, who had been buried nearly 24 years ago. The drizzle had started and one of my cousins held an umbrella over me. The coffin was lowered slowly into the cavity. My little cousin Elijah, who had not long been to his own Grandfather's funeral, came and stood by me. Granddad adored Elijah. I put my arm around him and said:

"It's just not fair is it, babe?" He looked up at me and shook his head.

"Ashes to ashes, dust to dust".

I looked behind me and saw Alex, standing from a distance, watching. I walked over and said hello to him, I thanked him for coming along, He said the service was lovely. His eyes were filling up with tears he had been trying to hold back for so long.

"I'm going to go now, before I get too upset," he said.

I appreciated his honesty. He didn't want to cry in front of anyone and decided not to come to the wake afterwards.

People laughed and reminisced over the pictures I'd put up in the pub. The food was eaten, a lot of us got drunk. It's all that could be done. Granddad got the send-off he deserved and I knew he would have liked it. After going home and having a nap I met up with my cousins later in Rochester and carried on drinking to continue the celebration of his life and the commiseration of his death. I laughed and joked about the times we had and my cousin Carl mentioned that exactly two months before his death, at my Uncle Ashley's wedding, Granddad made Carl promise to look after me if anything were to happen to him. I also discovered a few days after he died, when I was going through some of his things, that he didn't reorder his prescription medication, something he was always on top of. Maybe he'd finally had enough of living? Maybe he wanted to die, or maybe he knew his time was up. It seemed too coincidental; from saying what he did to Carl, to now.

Midnight arrived and I was pretty drunk on alcopops. I became overwhelmed with sadness and decided to get a cab home. I held back my tears until I put the key in the lock of my door. I ran up the stairs to my living room and flopped onto my sofa. I wept and rocked back and forth. I thought again about how Granddad died on his own. About how I left him in that hospital bed to go home. I was wracked with guilt. I said out loud again and again:

"I'm sorry, I'm so sorry, Granddad" I carried on until I must have fallen asleep.

September came and I proceeded to go to Granddad's grave every day and cry convulsively. Every day I'd say:

"I'm sorry, I'm sorry."

When he was alive, I would visit Granddad in between work and take him shopping, or to the hospital for checks with eye doctors and rheumatologists. Now I had a lot more time on my hands and hadn't realised that there would be a void I didn't know how to fill. I felt I had no purpose. I missed him. I knew that something had to be done to change it.

I had a plan. I planned to die on Christmas Day, that year, in 2004. A day when, due to others being with their families, I could do what I wanted to do to be with him, without anyone realising, without anyone interfering. I had three months to go and I knew it would fly by. I felt so unwanted now he had gone. So unloved. So uncared for. Ridiculously consumed with loneliness. And then something else happened.

I met Tyler…

31
TYLER

My birthday in 2004 was the hardest I'd faced. I cried all day. Not seeing my Granddad, or receiving a card from him was heart wrenching. Two months had passed since he'd passed and still life was no easier. Still I stood by his graveside any day or night I had spare saying:

"I'm sorry, I'm sorry,"

and still I longed for Christmas Day to arrive so I could finally alleviate the pain.

I found work hard, yet at the same time it kept me occupied. Late September I'd started supplying dancers Tuesday to Friday, to a club

Tyler

half an hour from me called Honour. I worked the odd shift there alongside my girls. Friday nights were generally busy, but the rest of the week was a lot quieter, which resulted in the dancers sitting around and talking amongst themselves a lot.

"Have you seen that dark haired doorman?" asked Carmen, one of my dancers that I'd trained up from my Academy "He's *well* fit."

She pointed him out. He was around 5'7", with a stocky build, dark hair and a square jawline. The other girls agreed with her, while I just thought he was "alright." As the month progressed, he would sit down with us all when there were no customers and join in with our conversations. His name was Tyler. He was married, with a two-year-old daughter. I'd talk about the modelling I did and the TV Channels I had worked on. He talked about his wife who used to be a dancer and wanted to be a model.

At the end of each evening Tyler would walk the girls and me to my car (as I was the designated driver) to make sure we were safe. He would always carry my stripper case. I always seemed to bring a bigger bag than everyone else. Habit, I guess.

Three weeks passed and one night, whilst walking Carmen and I to my car, Carmen asked Tyler if he would carry her bag too.

"No" he replied. Carmen and I looked at each other, miffed.

"Do you only ever carry Holly's bag then?" She asked.

"Yes" and he smiled at me. His mean look soon turned to a gentle one.

After loading the car with our bags and Carmen getting in, I gave Tyler a kiss on the cheek.

"I fancy you and *you* don't even notice" he said, in a grouchy tone, "why do you think it's only *your* bag I carry?"

I was speechless. For weeks all I had in my head was losing Granddad. I had no thoughts of wanting to even get close to anyone. And to be honest, I was always useless with recognising if someone was truly attracted to me. I think it's because of the dancing; people would look at me all the time at work and give out drunken compliments. I guess I never saw beyond that.

"I don't get involved with married men. See you next week."

I got in my car and drove away.

Tyler

> "You lucky cow" said Carmen "Typical, he picks the girl
> who's least interested in him!"

The following week as I began to spend more of my nights working
at Honour, Tyler's life began to unravel. Things were not great at
home. He'd been living in a volatile relationship with Gemma from
the start. I have no idea why he married into a relationship like that.
I guess he thought, like many of us do, that once that ring is on the
other person's finger, it's a fresh start and people will change. But
as those of us who get married know, and much to Tyler's dismay,
his wife didn't. I learned she was manipulative, and basically knew
how to press Tyler's buttons to wind him up and make him angry.
She was violent when she didn't get what she wanted and he had
bruises and scratches to prove it. On one occasion he slept on the
sofa and she woke him up by throwing cold water over him. She had
an injunction to keep him away from her and their daughter Grace,
but Gemma still had Tyler living with them as and when she felt like
it, encouraging him to break the law. He would live on other
people's sofas because Gemma would throw him out of the house
from one month to another, or bolt the doors from the inside
knowing that he wouldn't bang on the door late at night and ask to
be let in in case he woke up Grace. On those nights he slept in the
car as it would be too late to call anyone if he could stay at theirs.

Phone calls in the middle of the day and night when Tyler was at work – "Grace is asking for you" – meant he would leave work, resulting in him losing various jobs. He told me he had a son called Ryan from a previous relationship and he hadn't seen him in years. He lived with that guilt and feeling of loss, and was so determined for it not to happen again he would go to extremes for Grace, even if she was just "asking after him" and there was nothing seriously wrong.

Tyler knew he was being physically abused from time to time, but seemed unaware of the mental abuse. Screams down the phone from Gemma on voicemails when he was sleeping on someone else's sofa, because she couldn't get a hold of him, were verging on the ridiculous. I heard some of them one day – it was like a child having a tantrum. To me, the woman had serious issues. His co-workers and friends at Honour said he had been going through it for years with her and they kept advising him that it wasn't "normal."

I felt for him. Our in-depth conversations brought us closer together. I was starting to become attracted to him as I began to see the real Tyler beneath the hard exterior. He wanted to know about me, but I was not so open. All he knew was that my Granddad, who was like a Dad to me, had died a couple of months ago; that I had been married before and Martin and I were still great friends, and that the last guy I was dating (Kevin) had cheated on me. That was all I really

Tyler

gave away. But I let him talk and open up to me; something he apparently hadn't done with anyone before.

On my night off one Tuesday I went out with some friends of the management for a meal. All the other girls had to work as we were short staffed; so after a really wonderful à la carte dinner, I persuaded the guys to finish our evening off at Honour so they would spend money on the girls who couldn't get the night off to come out.

When we arrived, it was quiet, so the girls were more than pleased with me bringing in customers. Tyler was on the ground floor minding the door. When everyone on the top floor of the club were engrossed deep in conversation I decided to go down and keep him company. It was nearly midnight so Tyler was locking up; they stopped letting people in at that time on a weeknight. He looked sheepish as he reached for his jacket over the front desk and asked me:

> "Look, I'm just going to come out and ask this, are you involved with any of those men you came in with?"

> "Don't be stupid" I said, "they're mates with me and the other dancers here."

I'd pressed the button to call the lift to take me back to the third floor.

"Besides, why would I be involved with either of them..." I asked, as I stepped into the lift. "…when it's you I like."

I smiled coyly as I looked at him and he smiled back. As the lift was closing, Tyler ran into it, dropped his jacket on the floor and kissed me. I kissed him back passionately as he held me in his arms and I could feel his hard muscles through his crisp white shirt. He was the first person I'd really let hold me since Granddad died. I needed the care and attention from Tyler, and he needed me. We kissed like we would never see each other again. We spent the next 10 minutes just pressing the button in the lift to go up and down in the building, so that no one would see us; we didn't want the other staff to know about our little tête à tête.

After several repetitions of ground to third floor and third floor to ground, I finally went back upstairs to see everyone.

"Where have you been?" they asked.

"Oh, I just got chatting with Tyler downstairs, he was all on his own down there."

Tyler

Nobody suspected a thing.

The next few nights after, he would walk me to my car carrying my case and we would have a sneaky goodbye kiss. I told him I wouldn't go any further than that because he was still living with his wife and I did not want to be the other woman, no matter how much I liked him. I'd made the mistake of putting myself in that position in my early 20s, and it had gotten really messy for everyone in that triangle. I told myself never again after that relationship, and I had stuck with that advice I gave myself.

Every day I thought about Tyler. I looked forward to going to work, knowing that I would be seeing his face. I had to look disinterested in front of the others in case they suspected and wouldn't want us working together, but inside I was full of excitement. My life no longer seemed so meaningless now I had met him.

On a sunny Sunday in November, I was returning from Brighton, following a night out for Claire's birthday. My phone rang. It was Tyler.

"Gemma locked me out last night. I've decided not to go back."

"Are you *sure* you don't want to try and sort things out with her?" I asked, double checking.

"Nope," he said, "there's no point. She'll only do it again, and I'm fed up with her behaviour. I want to be with you."

I was elated. *Finally* Tyler had started to see sense. I couldn't stop smiling, knowing that he had made a great decision.

The following afternoon he drove to my house to see me. Opening my front door, he was grinning from ear to ear. He stepped inside and picked me up. I wrapped my legs round him and he spun me around, whilst we both smiled, and kissed one other. It was like the ending to a perfect chick flick with the happy ever after tagline. We were so happy that day. For him, it was one door closing and another opening, on a relationship that would be much less draining. For me, it was what I needed. Someone to spend some time with, and use up the spaces in the timetable of my life where I'd cry and plot my death for Christmas Day.

Every morning at 9am, when he was on his break from work (he was a labourer by day), he would always ring me, which would lift my spirits immediately for the day. I could always hear in his voice when Tyler was smiling. In the evenings after his day job and before his door job, he would still go and see Grace. I admired that in him.

373

Tyler

A man who still wanted to see his daughter; oftentimes I'd seen fathers walk away from all responsibilities. It broke his heart to have to leave her each night, but I told him that she's only sleeping in the evening, so he shouldn't feel bad. And with her being only two years old, him not being there full time because he no longer lived there would be something that Grace would get used to. She will be just as happy to see her Daddy even though he's no longer living with Mummy.

His greatest fear was losing his daughter if Gemma met someone new.

"I don't want another man in the house with my daughter," he would say.

I reassured him that no man could replace him because he's her Daddy. He worried a lot. It made me wonder what things Gemma would say to him to plant doubts in his head, as sometimes after he'd seen her, his mood would be much lower than before. Once with me though, he generally cheered up pretty quickly. He would always say:

"You're a breath of fresh air, Holly; I wish I'd met you sooner, and before I met Gemma."

"Yes, but if that had been the case, you wouldn't have had Grace. Only you and Gemma can make Grace, we would have had a different child. We all meet someone for a reason, and maybe that's why you and Gemma were meant to be together, just to make Grace."

"So why have we met now then?" He asked, questioning what I had just said.

"I haven't just met you now though," I replied "I feel like I've known you all my life and beyond. It sounds crazy, but I feel like I've met you in a past life too."

"I know what you mean because I feel the same thing," he said.

"Do you know what that means?" I asked "People that meet each other in every life they have?"

Tyler shook his head.

"It's called being soul mates. It means, that *we're* soul mates."

He smiled and nodded

Tyler

"Yep, I think we are."

Within just two weeks of being "officially" together, I became quite attached to Tyler. We still hadn't told anyone at Honour because we didn't want them breaking us up at work and wanted to prove that we could still work together professionally. Only one of his friends from work knew and only one of mine knew (Kyla). It was good to be able to confide in somebody, and I knew Kyla would keep her mouth shut. I didn't need to tell Carmen because she was having some time off, so the goodbye kiss at the car at the end of every night went unnoticed by the other staff.

Gemma was a real attention seeker. When Tyler stayed at my house, it was a good job he switched his phone off; in the mornings he would retrieve more voicemails where she would be screaming profusely down the phone, calling him names, saying she was lonely...the list went on. She should have thought about that before she mistreated him, I thought. Phone calls to Honour would occur when Tyler was working. The office phone would ring and ring and when the manager answered it, Gemma would hang up. For hours on end she would do it when Tyler wouldn't answer his phone to her. Tyler would angrily say:

"Wait 'til I see her tomorrow."

I explained to him that because he wasn't giving her any more attention, she was hoping for any kind of reaction from him.

"Any attention is better than no attention." I said to him "So if she's not getting it through hugs and kisses, she'll play the other card and hope for an argument. Don't stoop to her level."

He listened to me. He couldn't believe it worked. When she realised she wasn't getting anywhere with her tantrums, she calmed down. Gemma didn't know we were together yet. I didn't particularly want her to know as it was too soon and I didn't want it to cause problems for him seeing Grace. It was highly likely that she would have put a spanner in the works for him to see her if she knew.

I met Grace pretty early on. It wasn't particularly planned, but Gemma wanted to go out one morning when Tyler was on his way to mine and asked him to look after her that day. I was still in bed when Tyler let himself and his daughter in. I was awoken by her next to my bed. She was the prettiest thing I'd ever seen. I needn't have worried about how she'd take to me. She found a notepad and pen on my dressing table and she brought it over to me, sat on my bed and simply said:

"Draw."

Tyler

So there I sat, with little Grace beside me whilst I drew pictures for her. Tyler was amazed about how friendly she was with me. Usually she was dubious of people at her first meet. Children can usually sense good things, and I think that because her Dad was calm and happy around me, she knew she could feel safe.

After a few weeks, we decided to tell the staff at Honour that we were together. There was a mixed reaction. My dancer friends were happy for me, including Mandy, the girl who managed us. At least, that's what she'd said to me. The Doormen, being doormen, didn't have much to say and just hoped that Tyler could still do his job when he's working in the same venue as his girlfriend. He pointed out to them that he had been with me for a few weeks and that they hadn't noticed any change in his work ethics, so proved to them that he could still function around me without distractions.

But one night at work, he was told he couldn't work on the same floor as me anymore because it was "unprofessional". Mandy had said that the owner of the Security company had made that decision and that it was stupid, because we worked together so well. Little did I know then that it was Mandy who set the rule. She would say one thing, but be doing another. I started to notice that when she would talk about the other dancers to me, yet say something completely different to their faces. Stories she told didn't add up. I continued working upstairs lap dancing, while Tyler worked downstairs in the main part of the club (it was a nightclub downstairs at weekends and a strip club upstairs).

Tyler finally managed to get his own place to rent, so he didn't have to sleep on friends' sofas anymore. We took it in turns to stay at each other's house as he lived 40 miles from me, so it was only fair that we shared our journeys. He started to train in the gym again, something he hadn't done in a while, and felt better for it. And I could see it really helped him.

I bought him some things for his house as he had walked away from everything in the former matrimonial home. Just a few things like glasses, mugs, tea towels and cutlery. When I rang to tell him that I'd bought him some "housey" stuff, the reaction I received was not as I had expected.

"Don't buy me things!" he said in a raised voice "I don't want your help."

"Don't be silly," I laughed, "it's only a little something."

"I don't care! Take them back!"

I began to get upset:

Tyler

> "No I *won't* take them back. I'm not driving all the way back to the shops just to return a few gifts because you're ungrateful." I hung up.

I like doting on people, I've always been a big gift giver. I was taught don't give to receive and so from the day I could afford to buy presents for people with my pocket money, I would. Granddad wasn't around anymore, so me buying Tyler a few things made me feel like I was being helpful. After his stroppy phone call, I lay down on my bed and sobbed.

> "Never mind. I thought. Christmas is around the corner so everything will be alright then. I'll be with Granddad, someone who *does* want me around."

Tyler apologised to me later that day and explained that he's very independent and not used to people buying things for him. I kind of understood, as by the sound of it Gemma did nothing but aggravate him, and he wasn't very close to his father or stepmother. In fact, the only members of the family he would really talk about were his Uncle John and one of his brothers.

Two weeks before Christmas, Gemma tried to play a wild card for Tyler. Again, waiting to see how easily she could vex him, she decided to leave the house before he arrived one day so that when he opened the door, he could see that Grace was on her own –

entertaining herself and playing with a tin of shoe polish. Tyler, like any parent would be, was furious. He cleaned Grace up and put her in the car. It was at this time that Gemma returned, pretending not to understand why he was losing his temper.

"How can you leave a two-year-old on her own in the house?!" He screamed.

Gemma got in his car and refused to move, until he pulled her out by her wrist, then drove to the police station to explain what had happened.

When he rang me to tell me what had happened, I couldn't believe that a mother could be so uncaring towards her own child, just to cause an argument. Tyler was waiting for the police and Social Services to get back to him whilst in the meantime he could keep Grace with him overnight. I said if he needed it, I'd be happy to help him. If he could have custody of Grace that would have made his day. Alas, the hopes that he had were short lived, and due to the legal documentation Gemma had already put into place of him not being allowed anywhere near their home, Tyler's case was completely hopeless.

"I have to give her back" he said.

Tyler

He sounded so defeated and sad. I couldn't believe that Social Services would allow for Gemma to have her back that easily.

Claire was staying at mine that day:

> "If he needs anyone right now, it's you, Holly. Go and see him before work and I'll meet you there later."

I drove to Tyler's. He held me so tight. He was so unhappy.

> "I'm glad you've come to see me. I'm so glad I have you."

He gave me a bottle of perfume as an early Christmas present. It was two weeks until Christmas. Not long until I was planning to end my life; and Tyler had given me my present early, as if to say "use this while you can."

I didn't know what to do. It was still early days for Tyler and me, and I only had two weeks to either end my life or carry on. What would he do if I chose death over him? His words of "I'm so glad I have you" rang in my head. He kept saying he wanted to spend Christmas with me although I thought he may need to spend it with Gemma to see Grace, which I understood. In my eyes, children should always come first. Even though Gemma tried to annoy him by saying that he wouldn't be able to see Grace on Christmas day (also Grace's birthday), I guessed she would change her mind at the last minute, so Tyler would have to quickly cancel any other plans.

I wrote no Christmas cards that year, nor did I put up any decorations. As far as I was concerned, it was not time for a celebration. I'd always spent Christmas with my Granddad, since I was 14 months old. For years he had played Father Christmas for Schools and Retirement Homes and all for free. He had the long white hair and beard and owned a red suit he had especially made for the season. Christmas was Granddad's time. Everything reminded me of him.

Dealing with anything on the build up to Christmas was proving difficult, so when the Cellar Bar told me over the phone they wouldn't be using my agency anymore, I didn't even try to argue it. Was I disappointed? Yes of course, I'd had that contract for nearly two years. But truth be told, I asked myself what was the point if I may not even be around in a few weeks? Even so, I turned up at the second to last shift to collect my commission and to pick Claire up when she finished her shift. Todd the owner was extremely drunk and Claire said he had been a nightmare all evening – being overly mouthy to the girls saying:

"I'm the fucking Don of this place, you'll all do as I say."

Tyler

It was a Sunday night and he'd decided to have a blue night at lunchtime, followed by my girls afterwards. Having a day like that would prove difficult for the dancers on the latter shift. The idea is usually to have tamer girls on first, ruder girls after. Even when I worked at stag shows I was the warm-up girl in preparation for the blue girls. Why would the guys want the starter after the main course? It was on what should be one of the busiest days before Christmas but my girls struggled to get money out of the guys for lap dances. Todd didn't care about what the girls made this weekend, it was all about the money behind the bar, and with his involvement in drinking games with the punters, not only was the bar earning, but he was a drunken mess by about 7pm. I arrived three hours later. I collected my fees from the girls direct and said hello to Todd.

"Can I have a word with you outside, Holly?"

"Sure." I answered.

I knew the situation would be unavoidable, especially now he was intoxicated. Todd sat down on the wall:

"I guess you're wondering why we've decided to let you go and do it ourselves?"

"Well, yes, but the only thing I can think of is that it's to do with the pub over the road?"

He nodded:

"Exactly that. You told me it was tough shit that you were taking it on."

"Todd, that's not true, what I said to you was if I didn't take it on someone else would and you wouldn't know what was going on in there if that happened."

"*You* said the place was nothing to worry about, but *I* know they want to open every night as a strip club –''

"Yes, and I told him that it wouldn't work as people don't have that sort of money down here for the venue to turn a profit. Todd, I even let you choose the girls you wanted *and* gave you suggestions on how to make more money on the nights they were opened and you said you were doing really well from it. The girls hardly make any money there the days it is open, which is why I'm only using local girls -"

"-Bullshit, Holly! Utter Bullshit!" He began to raise his voice aggressively.

Tyler

"I don't understand which bit you're telling me is bullshit?"
I asked, confused. "I thought we'd sorted this?"

"Exactly, *you* thought. *You* didn't give a shit, hiding things
from me about the venue. They've put a pole in and we don't
have a pole-"

"And what? They've put a pole in on a platform with a 45-
degree angle that no one can stand on and isn't even in the
dancing area! You've never had a pole and it's never stopped
the clientele coming in nor the girls making money."

"Bullshit! Complete Bullshit!"

Bullshit seemed to be his favourite word at the moment yet he was
still making no sense, and making me out to be some sort of
backstabber.

"I told you from the minute I got asked to take that venue on,
Todd, that you and your bar would take precedence. I swear
on my Granddad's grave –"

"I don't want to hear about your *fucking Granddad*, I'm sick
of hearing about your *fucking Granddad*."

Todd knew nothing about my Granddad except he had died and that was why I visited less often to collect my fees. Todd was not a close friend, so did not know the ins and outs of my loss. All I was trying to do was swear upon something important to me to prove I was telling the truth. And the cold, harsh response I received shocked me. With tears in my eyes and a feeling of disgust towards what he'd just said to me, all that was left to say was:

"Fine. Think what you want. Good luck with it all."

And I took a couple of deep breaths to compose myself, walked back into the venue, wished my girls a Merry Christmas and told Claire I'd wait in the car for her. I never wanted to ever speak to or see that man again. And once Claire got in the car and asked what he'd said to me, she said she never wanted to speak to him again either, let alone work for him.

I worked Christmas Eve at Honour; even though I guessed it wouldn't be busy, just to give me something to do, and to see Tyler as he was also working. He was working on the ground floor but he popped up a couple of times in the night as even the nightclub was quiet. I hugged him and wished him a Merry Christmas. He could sense there was something wrong with me as I seemed pretty quiet. I didn't want to let him go. I felt safe when he held me. Safe from the world and from myself. Safe from the dark dismal despair I had felt since August. For the brief moments he would hold me, I forgot about 25th December being my last day to live. Yet at the same time, I wondered if this would be the last time he would ever get to hold me.

I finished work early that night and Tyler rang me when I got home to see if I was ok and said he'd call me in the morning to possibly arrange to come and see me. He was the only reason I switched my phone on that morning. I didn't want to talk to anyone else and I was still undecided as to what to do.

> "I can't see you today because Gemma said I can spend Christmas with Grace."

Just as I had suspected. But it was ok. That morning I realised I loved Tyler, even though I didn't want to tell him because it was too soon. Although Christmas Day was awful for me, I knew I didn't want to put Tyler through the pain of what I was feeling; I didn't want him to grieve for me, like I did over my Granddad. I knew he felt for me and I knew he needed me.

That Christmas, Tyler saved my life without knowing. Claire even says to this day:

"If you hadn't met Tyler, I truly believe you wouldn't be here now."

And she's right.

32

HAPPINESS AND HEARTBREAK

Between Christmas and New Year, Tyler and I spent time together at home, laying on the sofa and watching movies. We were content with what we had. I liked being at home and cuddled up to him. When we weren't watching TV, we were listening to music as we both had a love for rock, namely the hair metal sub-genre we had both grown up listening to. We would send each other apt lyrics when we were apart and one day after he quoted the chorus and bridge of Angel by Aerosmith to me, he decided to call me *his* Angel.

However, as we entered the new year, things began to change. Tyler's temper had started to alter and he'd begun to take steroids a few weeks prior. He would snap at the smallest things. He accidentally crashed his car into a motorway barrier on the way home back from mine one day and it was a write off. I felt guilty and partly responsible. So when he asked me if he could borrow some money to buy another car, I felt obliged to say yes. He knew my Granddad had left me some money, so I was unable to say I wasn't good for it.

"I'll pay you back £100 a week when I get my wages from doing the door work," he said.

I was going to Vegas the following day with Kay, who I knew from when I worked on the Girl Channels. We decided to go during the AVN convention together and have a bit of a girl's trip. I dropped the money off to Tyler beforehand so he could arrange to get a car when I was away. I saw the buckled barrier he had crashed into en route to his and I felt even guiltier. I also let him borrow my car during my Vegas break until he found a replacement. That day, he said those three little words to me:

"I love you."

He made my day, my week, my year and it was only January.

I went to Vegas knowing that when I came back, I had a man waiting for me, who loved me as much as I loved him and it felt wonderful. Kay and I boarded the plane to Vegas. We didn't actually know each other that well, but we pretty much clicked straight away when we first met on screen. Both of us were a little concerned as to how well we'd get along, but I knew it wouldn't be as bad as when I went away with Josh and breaking up after a week of being in each other's pockets. Kay and I were only going for four days.

She was feeling like she was getting the start of a cold on the flight so dosed up with cough mixture by sipping it occasionally as she had nothing to measure it out with. By the time we landed in Vegas, she had drunk half the bottle.

After a quick nap in our hotel we showered, slapped on some makeup and met up with my agent Rachel and her friends in a nightclub. With a couple of drinks in us, Kay was as high as a kite from the cocktail of cough mixture and vodka. We stayed out for a few hours until the journey had beaten us. We collapsed into bed, with Kay pretty comatose.

Tyler and I rang each other every day and continued to send text messages with lyrics to more rock ballads. He sounded like he was really missing me. It was the same with Kay and her boyfriend. We had both left behind lovesick men, yearning for our return. But that didn't stop us from having fun.

We walked around the convention during the day and lunched with Rachel, I napped a little as jet lag once again didn't agree with me and Kay went off to chill in the hotel spa. We got on well because we didn't stay in one another's pockets the whole trip. I bought a sequinned gown from a hotel boutique to go out in that night as it was AVN awards night, and despite not having tickets, we still wanted to look the part out and about. Kay wore a pinstripe trouser suit and bow tie, a little unconventional as all of the girls on awards night wore dresses, but it suited her. As we walked out of a restaurant in one of the hotel complexes, we turned heads as we looked like a couple. Kay played up to it:

> "Check this out" she said, getting down on one knee in the large open foyer as if to propose.

> "You're not funny," I laughed, hitching up my dress and running off to the escalator, giggling, part embarrassed, leaving her laughing on one knee whilst I shouted:
> "I'm not marrying you!" from the escalator. People thought we were for real; we made a great double act.

From that moment on, Kay always called me "Mrs." She even gave me a ring to wear on my wedding finger, which I actually did for some time. She was a real joker, and when we were put together we could entice most people into doing anything.

We got a taxi back to our hotel that night, drunk. The taxi driver made small talk in the cab and Kay sat in the front.

"Why have you come to Vegas?" he asked.

"We're here for the porn convention." I said.

"Oh!" His eyes lit up. "Are you porn stars?"

"Yep, all the way from England." Kay said. We didn't get into any small print because it didn't matter.

"I love porn." The cab driver said. Lame, but Kay pretended it wasn't.

"I bet you get all hard when you watch it, don't you?" She asked.

"Hmm" he muttered, now embarrassed. We stopped at some traffic lights.

"Are you going to get your cock out and show us how hard you get when you watch porn?"

My eyes widened in disbelief. This was not something I wanted to be a part of as I knew Tyler would flip, but I also wanted to see how persuasive Kay could be. Thank God I was in the back, so I could actually say I couldn't see fully. He looked at her coyly and giggled. The lights turned green and Kay continued talking to him gently, with her arm stretched out to the back of his seat. By the time we reached our destination he put the car into park and unzipped his fly. Kay leant over towards him, looking into his eyes.

"Go on, that's it, touch it and get it hard…give it a stroke for me. Pull on that dick…"

He stared into her eyes and breathed a little louder whilst she smirked seductively and he continued to play with himself as she instructed. I leant forward and he thought we were both getting involved, but me being the killjoy I can be, gave him the money with a tip and said:

"Thanks for the ride!"

Kay and I jumped out of the cab as quickly as possible and ran into the hotel laughing our heads off. That poor cabbie still had his cock in his hand. Let's hope no one jumped in straight after us.

That had to have been the funniest night we had there. Alas the following day, we both woke up with a cold and spent our final night in Vegas in our hotel room ordering room service meals of chicken soup and ice cream and sleeping it off.

Our boyfriends picked us up from the airport and I stayed at Tyler's. I was still feeling pretty unwell. I'd bought him a silver bracelet from a Native American shop in Caesars Palace. It took me ages to choose, as I didn't really want anything with too many gems in and I wanted something unusual to symbolise our love. The store owner helped me select it. It had patterns engraved around it and Tyler's face lit up when he saw it. He couldn't wait to wear it. I'd also bought Grace a giant pink soft toy for her room as he had just started redecorating it for her and she loved pink.

I fell asleep for a while and Tyler went to Gemma's to go and give Grace her present. When he returned he was really upset. The temples in his head were throbbing as he clenched his teeth. He sat on the edge of the bed. Gemma had obviously wound him up. Nothing unusual there, but his head was bowed and I had to crouch down to look at his face.

"What's going to happen between us?" he said "What if we eventually want a baby and we can't because of me and my past? What if people try to say I'm an unfit father?"

He wasn't making sense and I'd no idea where this was coming from as talk of having a child was a little hasty.

"You're a great Dad, you adore your little girl" I said. "But I think you need to go and try to see your son too, as I really think not seeing him is taking its toll on you."

"But what if I won't be allowed?"

Still crouched down, I held his hand.

"Tyler, look at me" He finally made eye contact. "Now you listen to me; that bracelet I bought you symbolises our love together. You're my soul mate and I love you."

"I love you too" he said

"You, Tyler, are my eternity. I can't explain why I feel like this so quickly but I do. We can face everything together and if or when we have a baby eventually nothing will go wrong

398

because it will be loved and he or she will have Ryan and Grace as brother and sister and they will love it too."

He smiled. We had an early night and I fell asleep in his arms.

He got up for work early in the morning and kissed me goodbye. I left around 1pm to go home and spent the rest of the day on the sofa dosed up with flu tablets. I wasn't booked in to work until the following week. Tyler rang me that night when he was at work to see how I was and we chatted.

The next day (Friday), however, I didn't hear from him. He didn't reply to a text message or pick up or return my calls. I knew something was wrong.

On the Saturday he rang and I said I was going to come down and get my clothes that I'd washed and left at his to dry. He snapped at me.

> "Don't just assume you can come down here when you want without asking." His attitude had changed completely. "I'll bring your clothes up to you when *I'm* not busy" he said.

I was confused. I hadn't done anything wrong. When he left on Thursday morning to go to work, everything was fine after our talk the night before. The whole weekend I fretted and dreaded the worst. The man I loved wholeheartedly was beginning to push me away.

He waited until Monday at 10.30am to come and see me. He had my clothes in a bag and my CDs that he'd borrowed. He asked for his CDs back. Just like the Wednesday night, he wouldn't look at me; every time I tried to look at him, he would turn his head. He ground his teeth again so his temples throbbed, and opened and closed his hands into fists with nervousness.

"I don't want to be with you anymore," he said "I need some time to myself; I need to get away. I'm going to stay with my Uncle John for a while" …

33
THE AFTERMATH

Have you ever felt like the world could crumble all around you and yet you would still be standing there, unaware of everything beyond your little bubble? That's how I felt. It was just Tyler and I at that moment. I couldn't fight back the tears. I fell to my knees and begged him to stay, to not break up with me. I couldn't breathe, my head hurt. He gave me no explanation; he wouldn't say a word. He was emotionless. He just watched me cry. I remember my phone ringing and it wouldn't stop so I threw it against the wall. That was the first time Tyler had seen me angry and I think he was shocked, but what did he expect?

> "Don't worry, I'll still make sure you get your money each
> week."

Then he walked out and drove away. He left me in the silence of my
house and the sadness of my mind. I felt so alone.

That was it – no Granddad. No Tyler.

Nothing.

Nobody.

I rang Kay and Claire to tell them but I couldn't bring myself to tell
anyone at Honour. I wasn't due to go into work there until a few
weeks anyway as I was booked elsewhere.
Tyler rang me later that day to see how I was and to apologise for
upsetting me.

> "Your apology is too late. If you don't want to be with me,
> you don't want to be with me. I love you and you've broken
> my heart." I sobbed.

There was nothing more he could say to me. Only him telling me he
made a mistake and wanted us to get back together would have made
me feel better.

"Are you getting back with Gemma?" I asked.

"No, I just need time to myself"

I, on the other hand, did not need time to myself. I sat at home, listening to our songs, sending myself further and further into despair. I couldn't eat, couldn't sleep; and when I did, I would dream about him or my Granddad and wake up crying. The tears wouldn't stop. My anxiety got worse and I'd pace up and down the house; hoping every time the phone rang it would be him, or every time I heard a car it would be Tyler.

Two days later Mandy rang me to ask if I would show up at Honour for Baby's birthday (one of the dancers) on the Friday.

"I'm not sure, I'll have to see." I replied uninterested.

"Are you alright? You've not called me; you've been very quiet and Tyler's not been into work either."

I had to tell her:

"Tyler broke up with me. He's decided to have some time out at his Uncle John's."

The After Math

I tried to hold back the tears as I told her. I also told her that I'd lent him money the week before. She couldn't believe we had broken up:

"You two were so good together."

"Try telling him that," I said.

I did show up for Baby's birthday. It was only four days since Tyler and I had broken up and I had lost seven pounds in weight. On arrival at Honour everyone noticed. I didn't look myself. I could feel the Doormen staring and the girls hugged me with sympathy.

Mandy told me that she'd found out that Tyler was still working on the door, but in a different town that was nowhere near his Uncle's, and that he'd got back with Gemma. I had to go home immediately. I didn't want to cry in front of all the staff and customers. Once home I poured myself a large glass of wine and downed it as quickly as I could. On an empty stomach, it made me drunk straight away. I texted Tyler:

"I can't believe you lied to me. You're not at Uncle John's, you're still working on the doors and you're back with Gemma. I thought that after everything, you could at least be honest."

After staggering around in the bathroom to get to the cupboard for a packet of razors, I went back to the sofa to sit down for a while, but ended up falling asleep, with a razor in one hand and my phone in another.

At 4am I was awoken by my phone. It was Tyler. He began shouting at me:

> "*Who told you* I was working the door? Just because I'm working here doesn't mean I'm not staying at Uncle John's! I'm not back with Gemma; *who* told you that?!"

> "Mandy" I said, in my sleepy state.

> "Yeah, well I'm not, and anyway, what does it have to do with you now that you're back with Martin?"

> "What!?" I sat up straight.

> "Well, aren't you?" he questioned.

> "No! Martin and I broke up *years* ago. Who told you that bullshit story?"

> "Mandy told one of the Doormen"

The After Math

I was angry. I could see that Mandy was making up stories to the other Doormen so that they would tell Tyler. Whether she was doing it because she thought she was helping I didn't know, but it was adding fuel to the fire and I decided not to tell her anything in the future.

Drunk, unhappy, angry and emotional, I cried down the phone at Tyler. Unbeknown to him I had that razor in my hand. He'd shout at me and then I'd cry back at him:

"I'm sorry, I'm sorry, I miss you."

"I don't know what you want me to do, Holly" He sounded frustrated.

"Get back with me."

I whimpered, holding the razor to my upper arm, waiting for his response and hoping it would be the answer I wanted.

"Stop asking me, you know I can't be with you" He said furiously.

I pressed the razor into my arm and dragged it widthways across. Blood started to trickle out of my cut. I continued as Tyler carried on talking:

"It won't work between us."

Each time I made another cut in my arm I repeated out loud to him

"I miss you. I love you. I want you back. I'm hurting,"

watching the blood come out of every cut. But Tyler did nothing but shout at me. Did he not care? Or was he just shouting because he was angry with himself that he'd hurt me? I don't remember how the conversation ended. I still felt drunk and hysterical. I think he just hung up.

I knew I would do something stupid if I didn't call the Mental Health unit again at the hospital. On the Monday they paid me a visit and made me an urgent referral. They prescribed me Olanzapine to take with my beta blockers. Olanzapine, in high doses is used as an antipsychotic drug, but they had prescribed me a small dosage to help with my anxiety disorder. I never took it. I continued with the beta blockers and started reading self-help books to try and become more positive. The hospital also suggested I attend their relaxation technique classes, which showed you how to meditate.

Tyler rang me one more time that week to see if I was ok, to tell me he didn't have my money and to say he missed me. I said I'd always take him back "no matter when, no matter what" because he was my soul mate. But he never said he wanted me back and he changed his number after he rang so I couldn't contact him again.

I needed to get away. Abel mentioned there might be a job for me in The Hague in the Netherlands, running girls in a strip club, and decided to go over for the interview. It would be a permanent job so would have meant relocating. I had to fly to Amsterdam to see Abel to talk about it.

The day before my interview was Tyler's birthday. I bought him a card, found out where his Uncle John lived and put the card through the door. As I walked away, my heart beating faster because I couldn't believe I had done it, I heard someone shout out after me:

"Excuse me?"

I turned around. It was a man from the house. I walked back.

"You put this card through my door? I'm not Tyler."

"Are you Tyler's Uncle, John?" I asked.

"Yes"

"Tyler told me he was living with you for a while, so I wanted to put his birthday card through your door."

"No he's not and he hasn't been" he frowned.

Once again, Tyler had lied to me.

"Ok" I said, embarrassed by the whole situation. "My name's Holly and I was going out with Tyler for a little while;"

"Yes, I remember him talking about you" he interrupted

"Well, he broke up with me and has changed his number. He owes me money and I don't know how to get in touch with him."

Uncle John invited me in:

"I've got his new number somewhere."

He made me a cup of tea and asked some questions about me; where I was from and my background. He was annoyed Tyler had borrowed money from me. We chatted for over an hour. He seemed really nice and his views on life reminded me of my Granddad's, although Uncle John was much younger. He was a comfort to me after a month of being unhappy without Tyler and months of missing Granddad.

He gave me Tyler's number and he suggested I take Tyler's birthday card with me because he was sure that I'd be seeing him later once I rang him.

"Do pop round and see me again, won't you? It was lovely to meet you."

I left, smiling; it seemed I had gained an Uncle, even though Tyler wasn't my boyfriend anymore. Once I was back in my car, I dialled the number I had been given and Tyler answered.

"Hello?"

"Happy Birthday" I said.

"Who's this?" he asked. I could hear Grace in the background.

"Holly" I replied. He hung up.

I didn't ring him again; I left him alone, as I guessed he was with Gemma. When he finally returned my call, he didn't sound angry like I thought he'd be.

> "Uncle John told me he gave you my number. I'm sorry I lied to you, but I really needed time without you and didn't want you coming round to my place looking for me."

There wasn't much I could say to that:

> "I just wanted to get in touch with you to arrange for you to start paying some of my money back. What you've done regarding that is out of order." I said.

> "I know, Uncle John has told me off too. He's also told me he really likes you and that I should still be going out with you and divorce Gemma."

I felt smug. Only one hour of meeting Uncle John and he had already taken a shine to me.

> "Anyways," I said to him "I just wanted to give you your card before I go away and sort out how you're going to pay me back."

> "Go away?" he questioned "where are you going?"

"It doesn't matter" I said.

"No, *tell me* where you're going."

I hesitated, but he asked me again.

"I've been offered a job in Holland and I'm going tomorrow to see if it's worth taking."

There was a silence for a few seconds on the receiving end. Then he spoke:

"Look, I'm still living at my place. Can you come and see me tonight? Please."

I couldn't resist Tyler's request. At 6pm I drove to his house. I took some deep breaths before knocking on his door. I told myself to act strong even if I didn't feel it.

He opened the door. There he was, standing and looking back at me with the same smile that he'd always had when we were together. I hugged him.

"Happy Birthday" I gave him the card.

"I can't believe you remembered," he said.

"Why wouldn't I?"

We talked small talk about how we were both doing.

"The job in Holland sounds like it could be good for me. I'll be running girls over there and training them like I do over here. They're including a place to live."

Tyler appeared unsettled.

"Are you back with Gemma?" I asked him, hoping the answer was still no.

"No," he replied "we spend time together because of Grace but that's as far as it goes. We get on better when we're not together."

It was a relief to know that there was one thing he appeared to be telling the truth about; he broke up with me to have time to himself.

He looked me up and down:

"You look good" he said.

"Thanks" I smiled.

He stepped forward and kissed me. Something I didn't expect to happen but at the same time I'd hoped *would* happen. I reciprocated. Before I knew it, we were staggering to his room, holding onto each other, taking off each other's clothes and falling onto his bed. We made love. It was what I needed. For him to hold me one more time like he used to. But this time was a contrast from how we were before. I didn't lay with him after we finished. I got dressed immediately and showed no emotion. I needed to be the stronger one and hold myself together so I wouldn't break.

"You're different," he said.

"I'll see you around, okay?" I said to him, picking up my coat and made my way towards the front door.

I got as far as the kitchen door and Tyler shut it so I couldn't get out.

"What are you doing?" he asked, puzzled. "This isn't *you*; this isn't how you behave."

"What does it matter?" I said sternly. "You and I are over, I know that. Call what just happened closure."

I kissed him on the cheek and left. I was hurting inside so badly. I wanted to stay, wanted for him to hold me whilst I cried in his arms. But I didn't want to show him any weakness.

About two hours later he rang me.

"How long are you going to Holland for?"

"I'm not sure." I said "I have a one-way ticket."

"Well," he said "if you don't come back, I'll come and find you one day."

"Why would you?" I asked. "You're still married and have a child with her."

"Because one day, Holly, it will all sort itself out and I'll be able to be with you. I can't not have you in my life."

Whilst I'd craved for him to say that to me, I knew it was far from the truth; he could never look that far ahead, not with Gemma's behaviour, nor did I want to wait forever for him.
I couldn't wait to get on that plane. I took books to read and intended to see some of Amsterdam and try to relax. Being near water has always calmed me.

The After Math

The meeting went well; I just had to wait for the club to open. Abel hadn't given me an opening date, but he said in the meantime I could dance back at the club in Amsterdam where I worked at over the summer. My Doctor had advised me not to dance full-time for a while due to a hip injury. So after less than a week there, I came home.

Stupidly, I texted Tyler I was back when I was on the train home from Gatwick. Immediately my phone rang.

"So are you going to take the job?" he badgered me.

"I don't mean to be funny, but what has it got to do with you?"

"I need to know, that's all."

This made me think he'd reconciled with Gemma; perhaps he wanted me totally out of the picture.

"Yes", I replied, "I'm going to take it."

"Well I meant what I said, I will come and find you someday."

416

"There's no point in doing that." I said, biting my lip.

"Well I will, whether you like it or not. I'll talk to you later, I have to go" and just like that, he hung up.

I didn't speak to him again until I saw him at Honour when I went to visit the other girls. He was wearing his wedding ring. The straw that broke the camel's back. To know that everyone else would have seen that ring back on his finger before I did and not tell me was humiliating; and to know that he didn't have the decency to ring or text me to let me know himself was even more heart-breaking. I didn't know who to trust anymore. My dancer colleagues at work weren't keeping me informed; did they not realise they were hurting me? I felt so alone.

To expand Shimmer Agency, and to immerse myself in work while I was still unable to dance, I bought another agency called Stiletto Girls, from the owner who was retiring, for a nominal amount. She gave me boxes of contacts for venues and lists of girls. It all took me days to get through. I emailed or rang every girl on the list to expand my portfolio, which would in turn also generate interest in my agency from clubs and bars. I advertised on exotic dancing forums to attract new dancers.

The After Math

My usual insomnia had me up late checking my inbox. I received an application from a girl called Lisa. She was pretty in her pictures – blonde hair, lovely and slim. I rang her the next day.

Having plenty of dancing experience and being local, she couldn't wait to start work at Honour on the Tuesday. I agreed to meet her there the following night as I had meetings on her start date. Mandy said she did well on her first shift and worked hard, persevering to get dances.

When I met Lisa she was wearing a stunning long dress for work, the type we'd been taught to start our nights in when we worked in London, and her blonde hair was naturally wavy. We immediately built up a rapport. She was booked in for the rest of the week at Honour and I managed to get her a stag show for that weekend. Work was coming in thick and fast for my agency and I was pleased to give a fresh face the work she wanted. She seemed more driven than other girls on my books.

When I rang her one morning, she had said she'd had a sex dream about me. I laughed because I barely knew her but took it as a compliment. It wasn't every day that a girl said that to me.

Saturday arrived and I was longing for a night out. Lisa said she'd come to mine after the stag show in London and we should go to

Honour. I'd only ever worked there, so thought that a change of social scene might be good.

She got to mine around 11.30pm. By the time we got to the club it was 12. She'd driven from Kent to London for work, back to Kent to pick me up and then another 30 minutes to the club.

> "You've done loads of driving today, Lisa, I could have driven us here" I said once we reached the car park.

> "I'm fine, I'm not tired." She said reaching into her bag. "Besides, I've got this to keep me going." She pulled out a fake fingernail and what looked like a piece of paper and began to unwrap it. "Do you want some as a livener?"

Confused at the folded piece of paper, I asked:

> "What is it?"

She chuckled and replied:

> "Coke, babe. It's cocaine. Do you want some?"

34
GOING FURTHER DOWNHILL

If I could turn the clock back, I would have never gone out with Lisa. I often wonder if I had stayed in and stayed away from her, if I would have stayed away from cocaine for good. I knew plenty of girls who did coke (it's part and parcel of the job), but I'd only ever really seen it already made out as a line, never folded in anything like paper. I'd never wanted to touch it. The joints in Amsterdam were as far as I'd ever been with drugs. Occasionally I smoked a cigarette or drank alcohol, but that was it.

I knew Tyler took the odd line of cocaine with some of the other doormen or with Gemma. I guess I wanted to feel what he felt, and maybe if I took an interest in something that he did, he would again take an interest in me. How stupid could I be?

Now, here I was in a car, with cocaine scooped on a false fingernail, one finger pressing on the side of one nostril and the fingernail underneath the other nostril, sniffing hard to get that white powder as far up my nose as possible. I can't even say I particularly enjoyed the night as we were only out for a couple of hours. Lisa got lucky with one of the doormen in his car whilst I sat in her car next to them, with the engine running to keep the heaters on and the wrap of cocaine that she'd left me to "look after" to entertain myself. Her liaison was short-lived as a bar girl from the club spotted that they were at it, so they said their goodbyes and Lisa drove us back to mine.

Upon getting home, I had severe restlessness. I kept re-arranging everything on the coffee table.

"What are you doing?!" Said Lisa

All I could do was laugh:

"I don't know!" I replied. Lisa was laughing too.

"I think the powder's got to you, babe!"

She and I talked for hours, we were so wired. When I went to make her bed up, Lisa said she'd share with me to save the bother. We got ready for bed and as we started to get undressed she said:

"You know I liked you the minute I met you" and she looked at me suggestively as she moved in closer to me…

I couldn't help but kiss her. Lisa pulled me onto the bed. We laughed, joked, kissed and played with each other. We used nearly all the toys in my side draw. We even filmed the fun we had on my phone – it was the first camera phone I had. By the time we both reached orgasm, it was daylight and we fell asleep, with her legs draped over me.

I went back to work at Honour the following week and Lisa and I remained close. My wisdom teeth had started cutting through. The pain was unbearable and nothing seemed to alleviate it, other than a bit of baby teething gel, but I was using it far too often.

"Try putting some coke on your gums babe" said Lisa.

It worked. No more pain, for long periods of time. It was like a super-duper teething powder. And was I not only out of pain, but I was also high.

"That's an added bonus" I thought.

My other attraction to the drug was also that with cocaine I could drink more and not feel drunk.

The next month I worked, drank and snorted cocaine. I still missed Tyler tremendously. He worked back at Honour from time to time and if he heard a specific rock ballad playing, he knew I was dancing and I'd spot him watching me from the door. It was a ritual for Tyler and Gemma to break up pretty much every week and he was apparently still pretty miserable, but whenever he saw me, he smiled.

Honour was taken over by new owners and they soon put a stop to having lap dancers. They just wanted a normal night club. Lisa and I didn't see each other as much because we worked in separate venues.

One Friday after Baby had finished working a pub shift for me, we decided to go out. Because it had been a couple of weeks we decided to go to Honour to go and see all the other staff and have a few drinks. Much to my delight Tyler was working, as was Paul, who Baby had taken a shine too.

Tyler paid no attention to working the door and spent most of his time flitting around me and getting annoyed if other men spoke to me. I revelled in his jealousy. Baby went missing in the lift for a while with Paul, to get a kiss where nobody could see. Something I could relate to from mine and Tyler's mischief a few months before. Eventually Tyler and I ended up flirting with each other; I probably got him into trouble as I distracted him from his work, but I enjoyed having some time with him again, even in a nightclub. Because of the chemistry between us, I was convinced that he wanted me to see me after work. I sat on the pavement outside and waited for him. Baby lived close to the club and had managed to get someone to drive her home.

"Ring me when you get in," she said.

Tyler finally showed up.

"What are you doing here?" Not the reception I was expecting.

"Let me stay at yours. Please" I begged, drunkenly.

"No. I have to be up early in the morning" Again, not what I was expecting.

"Well then take me home and stay at mine, and get up early."

He raised his voice:

"Why do you always have to make things awkward for me!?"

I felt like I was being told off like a little girl. I held back the tears and bowed my head:

"But I…"

"I've not got time for this," he interrupted. "Now *go* home."

He got in his car and drove off, leaving me on my own in the car park. I walked back towards the club to see if anyone was around to give me the number for a cab.

I shed more tears on the street corner waiting for my taxi. I felt stupid.

The journey seemed like it took forever to get me home. I slumped through my doorway onto the floor and sobbed. I felt humiliated, making a drunken fool of myself in front of Tyler. This was the first time he'd seen me drunk. Again, I blamed myself for his behaviour, accusing myself of making him act like that. I played the songs we used to listen to and I started typing a letter on the computer. It didn't take long to say what I wanted, to who I wanted, despite being drunk I still managed to have the determination to type everything up pretty quickly. I saved it and titled it:

"To be read at my funeral."

Tyler didn't want me anymore. Nobody alive wanted me. I was a useless mess. I felt so unloved. I walked to the kitchen cupboard, pulled out a box of paracetamol, went to the sink and got myself a glass of water. I sat at my desk, took the pills out of the box and began popping them out of the blister pack. I counted them as I lined them up.

"One. Two. Three…"

There were 15 in the box. Was 15 enough?

"I could take some of the other pills in the medicine box just in case," I thought.

I stared at the tablets. Still crying, I re-counted them. Should I, shouldn't I? I cried and called out for my Granddad to help me. I wanted to be told why I should live or die. I just wanted to validate one of the options. I felt scared. I rang a suicide helpline, but the man said they're not allowed to give advice, just listen. I found it hard talking to them through my crying so I hung up out of frustration. Hyperventilating and crying, I took the first pill on the desk. I found it hard to swallow, my mouth dry from all the upset.

"One" I took some deep breaths to calm myself but it didn't work.

"Two" I gulped more water.

The phone rang. It was Baby. I answered:

"Hello"

"I wanted to make sure you got home ok because you didn't ring me. What's wrong?

You sound upset. Are you at home?"

"Yes."

"Did Tyler drive you?"

"No"

428

I was trying to breathe steadily so she could hear me through my tears. I told her what Tyler had said before he drove off.

"I'm so sorry; you deserve so much better than him."

"I didn't deserve for him to treat me like that. All I've ever done is love him" I said hysterically, "and I don't know what to do anymore."

"You're a beautiful person babe, don't let him get to you."

"It's too late, it doesn't matter anymore. Can you tell Claire to look on my computer, there's instructions on there." I had the third pill in my hand.

"What do you mean, instructions?" She sounded worried.

"Just tell Tyler I love him. I can't do this anymore, Baby," I sobbed loudly.

"Please don't do anything stupid. Holly, *please, please* don't."

All she could hear was my crying, but she continued talking to me:

"Whatever you're doing, or thinking of doing, *don't*. We all love you. You're a wonderful person. You deserve to be happy and have someone treat you like a princess. Don't let him do this to you."

"I'm so unhappy, Baby, I just want to be with Granddad now."

Baby started to cry too:

"I know, but we will all miss you, *please* don't. Have you done anything? Or taken anything?"

I told her I had the pills counted out on the desk and I had the third one in my hand.

"*Please, please* flush them away. Everything will be ok. We'll make it ok. Holly – *please.*"

Baby cared, and I believed her. She made me begin to realise at least just one person would miss me. After more begging from Baby and more hesitation from me, I scooped the remaining paracetamol into my hand as she instructed and walked to the bathroom. Still crying, scared of living, afraid of dying, I quickly let go of them over the toilet before I could change my mind and flushed them. I fell to my knees, sobbing, and told her I'd done what she'd asked.

"Thank you, thank you, I love you so much Holly," she said, relieved. "I can't get to you because I'm too far away but I promise to call you tomorrow."

Still drunk, my face sore from crying, I lay on my bed and wept till I fell asleep.

Like Tyler before, Baby had saved my life, even though this time I'd been one step closer. I will always be grateful to her.

35
A FRESH START

April came and I flitted between two men: Tyler would turn up at my house from time to time and we'd sleep together, and Simon, who I'd known for a while, would stay over on the odd occasion. Simon reminded me of Johnny Depp looks wise; but what went on in his head concerning me was a mystery. One minute he'd be saying the nicest things to me and the next, he didn't want to talk to me. Tyler wasn't much different. He didn't like me being around Simon, but I told him my life was nothing to do with him, seeing as he was still sauntering between Gemma and me. Tyler had changed his number and blocked it when he called me, so I never knew when I was going to talk to him. He came and worked for me around the house to pay off some of the debt he still owed, but everything was on his terms and never mine.

Claire broke up with her boyfriend and wanted to get away from her hometown, so I suggested she move in with me for a while. I needed the company.

Claire was carefree. Her attitude to life was amazing. Her sarcasm was of an even higher level than mine and she was always hyper. We had the same warped sense of humour. She lifted my spirits as soon as she moved in. Every day I laughed; even when I was upset, I still found it in me to smile some of the day. I wasn't hanging around Lisa anymore and Claire didn't even drink, let alone take drugs, so I didn't feel the need to take cocaine. One day I realised I hadn't taken my anxiety medication and I didn't have the tremors like I normally did when I forgot. I decided to see how long I could go without it. And it turned out I didn't need it again.

If Claire was working a different shift to me and I was home, I'd have her dinner on the table when she arrived back. If I was working and she was home, the house would be spotless when I returned. We went out together in the daytime to the shops; some evenings we'd go clubbing or to the pub, and people started to think we were a couple. On the odd occasion if one of us went out alone, people would ask:

"Where's your other half?"

We found this highly amusing and would go along with it, making out we were girlfriend and girlfriend, even though nothing sexual had ever happened between us, and neither of us wanted it to. We were like sisters and called one another soul sisters.

Claire was seeing a guy called Chris who was just as fun to be around; the pair of them always got on well with Simon too, so when the two boys stayed over, we'd stay up for ages chatting and laughing away. Some weeks I wouldn't hear from Simon, just like the Tyler scenario, which only made me feel more neglected, but at least I had Claire around.

I hadn't heard from Tyler for a few weeks, which was unusual, but I guessed things were going well with him and Gemma, albeit much to my dismay. I had booked a flight to Los Angeles for work, doing girl-girl porn, modelling and dancing. Rachel had liaised with a better agent this time, who would also provide accommodation for a small fee and was happy for me to just do girl-girl for them, as long as I paid my rent – for a room all to myself, rather than with three other girls. This agent was not one for trying to force girls into doing work that they didn't want to.

The weekend before leaving, Uncle John called.

A Fresh Start

"Tyler's been arrested."

Following an argument at home, Gemma had Tyler arrested by ringing the police and screaming she feared for her life. His bail conditions required that he wasn't allowed near the road of their matrimonial home. However, he needed to walk down that road to get his car to drive to Uncle John's; the address he was bailed to. Uncle John had told him to explain to a Police Officer what he was doing so he could collect his car, but the advice fell on deaf ears and a Police car drove by and spotted him in breach of his bail. The result was Tyler being arrested again the same day. Uncle John went to the police station to get him released.

"Can you come and see him at mine?" He asked.

I was prepared to leave the country for a six week break and here was Tyler, popping up in my life again, wanting support.
I saw him every day before I went away. We would sit in the car and talk. About life in general, Grace, his relationship with Gemma and me going to LA. I even drove him one day to see a counsellor about anger management – something the Police had recommended he do before his court hearing. The counsellor said they didn't think that he alone was the problem, and he was relieved about that.

Despite his bail conditions, Gemma rang Tyler towards the end of the week and cried for him to come home. Uncle John and I told him not to breach his bail but all he would say was:

"She's my wife" or "Grace needs me."

Once Tyler had an idea planted in his head, he would not budge. Tyler would only do what *he* wanted. Gemma treated him like a wounded animal; she would pet him and throw him a bone every so often, and then when he was comfortable she would then push him away and start a fight. She was now back to throwing him a bone stage and Tyler couldn't see the wood for the trees.

I left him to his own devices. I still loved him but refused to tell him anymore because it wouldn't help his situation or mine. After finally giving me the remaining money he owed, he drove me to the airport and I said I would call him to see how his day in court went, which was in a few days.

My working holiday was my new focus. A new country, sunshine and hopefully new friends. I boarded that plane on my own and for eleven hours sat with eager anticipation of what awaited me on the other side of the Atlantic Ocean.

Los Angeles, here I come…

ACKNOWLEDGEMENTS

Thanks to:

Andrew, for supporting me and introducing me to Antonia.

Antonia, who has been fantastic and helped me with every little worry I had with regard to getting this book out.

Ant M, for all the website advice and support.

Gareth my awesome editor, who always had faith in me, even when I didn't.

Stu, my darling brother, who gave me ideas and suggestions re my artwork.

Printed in Great Britain
by Amazon